# PARIS

# RENDEZ-VOUS

# PARIS

# RENDEZ-VOUS

## Where to meet in Paris hour by hour

### by Alexandre Lazareff

Translated by Joan Z. Shore

PRENTICE HALL PRESS
NEW YORK

This edition published by Prentice Hall Press
A division of Simon & Schuster, Inc.
Gulf + Western Building
One Gulf + Western Plaza
New York, New York 10023

PRENTICE HALL PRESS is a trademark of
Simon & Schuster, Inc.

Library of Congress Cataloging-in-Publication Data

Lazareff, Alexandre.
    [Paris rendez-vous.   English]
    Paris rendez-vous : where to meet in Paris hour by hour / by
Alexandre Lazareff : translated by Joan Z. Shore.
       p.     cm.
    Includes index.
    ISBN 0-13-650185-0 : $10.95
    1. Restaurants, Lunch rooms, etc.--France--Paris--Guide-books.
2. Hotels, taverns, etc.--France--Paris--Guide-books. 3. Paris
(France)--Description--1975---Guide-books.      I. Title.
TX910.F8L3913 1988
647'.954436--dc19                                      88-12510
                                                          CIP

No guidebook can ever be completely up to date, for
telephone numbers and opening hours change without
warning, and hotels and restaurants often come under new
management. While every effort has been made to ensure
that information was correct at the time of going to press,
the publishers cannot accept any liability for any
consequences arising from the use of information
contained herein.

# *Contents*

# Thanks

To my parents, closely associated with this research, who have guided me, corrected me, and expanded my taste for *rendez-vous*.

To Renaud Girard, whose crucial involvement got the project off the ground.

To Marie-Hélène Corbin, a real friend, who gave me the benefit of her writing ability.

To François Auque, Walter Butler, Olivier Farkas, Jacques Reiller, and Jean-Luc Soulé, who have looked over the manuscript.

To my guinea pigs—who have remained friends nevertheless—who for better and for worse participated in these long forays.

*In memory of Anne,*
*For those who keep her alive.*
*Mamy, my parents, Sonia.*

# Foreword

THIS SLIM GUIDE doesn't claim to be a complete compendium. It lists only those really good rendez-vous places and deliberately skips over the luxurious but passé bar, the popular but overcrowded tea room, the great restaurant whose highly touted cuisine is ruined by an off-hand, off-putting, and offensive reception.

A good rendez-vous place must meet certain criteria: it lets you wait in comfort, it answers your particular needs—business, seduction, or whatever—and it's open to everyone, which eliminates those clubs that may or may not let you in, or those here today, gone tomorrow nightspots that are no sooner "discovered" than they're deluged.

In addition, coming up with a geographical balance has sometimes forced me to make some difficult choices between two establishments of nearly the same quality. In such instances, I cite one of them as the "emergency alternative" to the other.

The specified time is when I feel the ambience is most characteristic. For example, it seems that Taillevent's discreetness makes it a perfect rendez-vous for lunch, while Chiberta's extraordinary elegance makes it better for evening engagements. Similarly, in the evening, Asian or provincial-style restaurants serve earlier than fashionable places, which cater to a late-night crowd.

# Introduction

If Proust were to write *Remembrance of Things Past* today, would he change the setting? His Paris, cocooned in plush parlors and private clubs, is passé; more and more, it seems that Parisians live outdoors—in cafés, bars, restaurants, and tea rooms.

Today, choosing the place for a rendez-vous requires great inventiveness, imagination, and knowledge based on solid experience. If you refuse to resign yourself to the monotonous round of drugstore counters, corner cafés, or other mundane spots, this guide is for you: it will help you find the place that is ideally suited to the person and the time of your choice.

For everything has its setting. The seducer's charm is enhanced in a warm, comfortable atmosphere that will help overcome the hurdles of love's obstacle course. The international businessperson will appreciate the hushed discretion of a distinguished gastronomical retreat to discuss the terms of a contract. The aesthete will be looking for elegant waiters, architectural beauty, and an attractive table setting. The snob will dumbly succumb to the latest fad, or fall for anything that looks "retro."

Also, every hour has its pleasures. It is the moral obligation of every true-blue (or aspiring) Parisian to find the right time for each appointment; to differentiate among the noontime, evening, and nighttime restaurants; to prowl knowledgeably among the midnight, late-night, and early-morning bars; to know which are the first nightclubs to hit, and the last.

Hour by hour, this timely guide will tick off the proper places for all your rendez-vous in Paris. It's not yet another gastronomic guide, nor a handbook for your social life, but rather a *vademecum* to help you make up your mind on the spur of the moment or the whim of the hour. Therefore each rendez-vous description is supplemented with a clear list of "instructions."

The French fondness for classification makes it imperative to give ratings. So I have awarded *coupes* for the atmosphere, the welcome, and of course, the quality of the cuisine, according to the following scale:

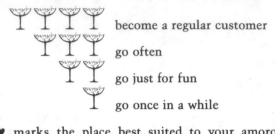

become a regular customer

go often

go just for fun

go once in a while

A ♥ marks the place best suited to your amorous adventures.

Last of all, for this new edition, the award for the Rendez-vous of the Year has been given to Le Jules Verne restaurant.
It's up to you now to have a good time. . . .

# Morning

*Breakfast*
*Brunch*

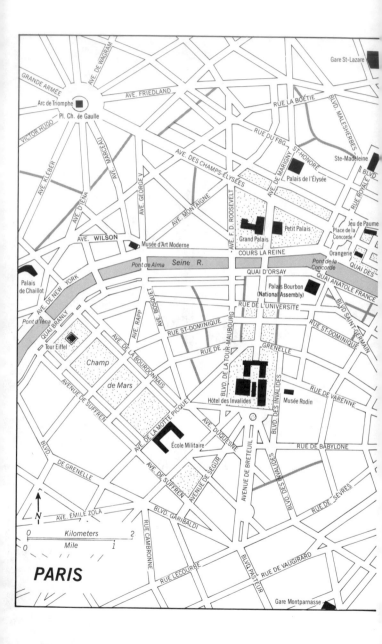

2 PARIS

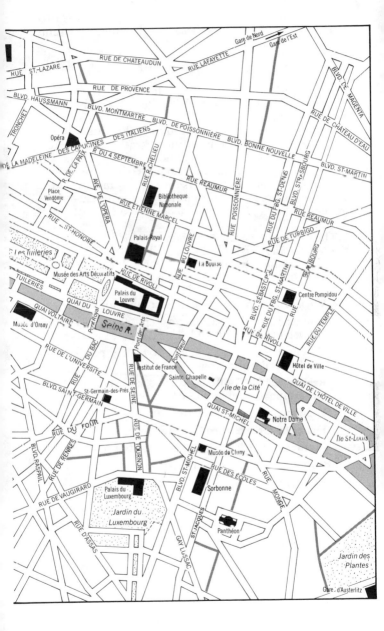

PARIS 3

# Le Cochon à L'Oreille

5 a.m.

"Bonjour, M'sieurs, M'dames. Not too warm today." The opening of Le Cochon à l'Oreille at 4:45 a.m. is like a curtain-raiser.

The aproned waiter has already polished his espresso machine, placed the tables out on the sidewalk, and dusted up inside. One by one, the butchers, bakers, and deliverymen of the neighborhood arrive—chatty and cheerful. One of them orders *un petit crème*, "filled to the brim, as usual," while another shouts, "Jean-Pierre, my *demi*" or "a *rillettes* sandwich and a glass of Côtes du Rhône."

The clown above the bar, the old wood benches from the Métro, and the mosaics—recalling Baltard's trolley cars and the old street markets—haven't changed for a century. It's as if Les Halles were still Les Halles.

- **With whom:** your nighttime companions.
- **Where:** 15, rue Montmartre, 1st. Tel.: 42.36.07.56. Between the Forum and rue Étienne-Marcel.
- **When:** from precisely 4:45 a.m. to 4:30 p.m.; closed Sunday and holidays.
- **Recommended:** coffee and croissant, the *rillettes*—potted meat sandwiches (if you can manage it).
- **Welcome:** a waiter straight out of central casting.
- **Dress:** butcher's apron or blue overalls.
- **Bottom line:** for the last coffee or the first drink.
- **Cost:** 10 F. for coffee and croissant.
- **Emergency Alternative:** Le Vaudeville (p. 178).

# Le Terminus Nord

7 *a.m.*

The pictures of greyhounds, racehorses, and motorcars make this 1925 *brasserie* look more like a drawing room in Deauville than a railroad station cafeteria.

Although Le Terminus Nord is not the first place to open in the neighborhood, it's the only place where you're not greeted grumpily in the early hours, where the homemade croissants are as good as those made next door at Mauduit, and where you can wake up gently, hunched over the friendly bar.

The railroad conductors, who come and dunk buttered toast in their *café crème*, have the right idea. It's even rumored that their colleagues from the Gare de l'Est make a special detour over here.

- **With whom:** your travel companions.
- **Where:** 23, rue de Dunkerque, 10th. Tel. 42.85.05.15. On the square of the Gare du Nord.
- **When:** from 7 a.m. to 12:30 a.m.
- **Recommended:** the homemade croissants, the buttered half-baguettes, the *café crème.*
- **Welcome:** friendly.
- **Dress:** for travel.
- **Bottom line:** a good way to avoid having an expensive breakfast on the train.
- **Cost:** 20 F.
- **Emergency alternative:** none; all the nearby cafés are horribly depressing.

# Les Deux Magots

Saint-Germain
Intellectual

Is this "the rendez-vous of the intellectual elite," as proclaimed on the menu? Somehow, if you need to announce it, you automatically cast doubt on such a claim.

Is it still a café for creative souls? The fact is, the two large statues of Chinese mandarins (the two "magots") no longer stir the imagination as they once did that of an earlier generation.

To tell the truth, this place is haunted, and it's amusing to watch people look for celebrities who are no longer around. Every time the revolving door turns, there's a sense of expectation . . . usually followed by disappointment. *Fini*—the days of Sartre and Simone de Beauvoir.

But if the glamorous image has faded with time, at least the spiffy waiters, fully aware of *their* image, manage to keep up appearances. And the big advantage of having breakfast at Les Deux Magots is simply this: you can sit and quietly read *The International Herald-Tribune*, or a soon-to-be-published manuscript, while enjoying a really good cup of coffee or an old-fashioned hot chocolate.

- **With whom:** a publisher, an author, a beautiful date.
- **Where:** 6, place St-Germain des Près, 6th. Tel.: 45.48.55.25. Facing the church of Saint-Germain-des-Près.
- **When:** from 8:30 a.m. to 1:30 a.m.; closed early January.
- **Recommended:** strong coffee (an *exprès*) or old-fashioned hot chocolate.
- **Welcome:** often haughty.
- **Dress:** stylish.
- **Bottom line:** the elegant, morning meeting place.

○ **Cost:** 50 F.

○ **Emergency alternative:** *Le Flore*, of course, on the next corner at no. 172. Tel.: 45.48.55.26. Renowned for its brioche toast and its scrambled eggs; readers of *The Financial Times* make a special detour.

# Le Vaudeville

8 a.m.

The big empty room, restored to order after last night's revelries, is again ready to greet customers. At the bar, polite but harried waiters can barely keep up with the stream of orders from French Press Agency journalists, all in a hurry to get back to their telex machines.

If you are more groggy and less aggressive than they, head for a table in the adjoining room where you can catch a glimpse through the window of the massive Bourse (stock market) building across the street.

You have just enough time to dip your croissant in your coffee before the day's trading begins.

- **With whom:** early-morning journalists.
- **Where:** 29, rue Vivienne, 2nd. Tel.: 42.33.39.31. Opposite the Bourse.
- **When:** every day from 7 a.m.
- **Recommended:** coffee and croissant.
- **Welcome:** friendly, but rushed.
- **Dress:** like a foreign correspondent.
- **Bottom line:** get the latest news.
- **Cost:** 15 F.
- **Emergency alternative:** *Café de la Paix*, 12, bd. des Capucines, 9th. Tel. 42.68.12.13.

# *Hôtel de Crillon*  ♥

Concorde
Showy

Diplomatic life isn't what it used to be, but the Ambassadors' Salon at the Crillon continues to maintain the illusion.

Imagine, for just a moment, His Majesty receiving the envoys of the King of Siam surrounded by the gilt, marble, and crystal chandeliers of this sumptuous palace designed by the 18th-century architect Gabriel, and greeting them with a preposterous meal of English sausages, papayas, and a creamy Saint-Nectaire cheese.

Must you really hold your business breakfasts here? Wouldn't you prefer to dazzle a woman by exploring the alluring prospect of a late supper served on the terrace of the Royal Suite?

- **With whom:** a business acquaintance, or better yet, a new acquaintance.
- **Where:** 10, place de la Concorde, 8th. Tel.: 42.65.24.24. Between the Automobile Club and the U.S. Embassy.
- **When:** from 7 to 11 a.m., in the Salon des Ambassadeurs.
- **Recommended:** take as much as your heart desires. Don't forget the English sausages, the cheese platter, and the fresh exotic fruit.
- **To avoid:** orange juice (it's not fresh), tea (in bags).
- **Welcome:** perfect.
- **Dress:** dark suit.
- **Bottom line:** a classy breakfast.
- **Cost:** 85 F.
- **Emergency alternative:** *Le Bristol* (p. 43). Also 16th-century style, but inferior in the pastry department. For this, someone deserves the guillotine.

# Le Plaza Athénée

## 9 a.m.

Like any typical American staying at the Plaza, you'll summon your French business associates to the hotel for a 9 a.m. business breakfast. In the good old days your French colleagues would have balked, but not anymore. As they too become workaholics, they're beginning to copy quaint American corporate customs.

The Plaza's impressive dining room, designed to impress the rich *bourgeoisie* of the Belle Époque, is the quintessential setting for a morning meeting: spacious, quiet, and elegant. The croissants and homemade preserves are delicious, the pastel tablecloths and flower arrangements are delightful, and the verdant view of the ivy-covered courtyard should lull your clients, collaborators, and competitors into utter compliance with whatever you propose.

- **With whom:** a harried executive.
- **Where:** 25, avenue Montaigne, 8th. Tel. 47.23.78.33. Next to the Champs-Élysées Theater, near the Alma.
- **When:** every day from 7 to 11 a.m.
- **Recommended:** the Continental breakfast, with scrambled eggs. Watch out for the extras that add up: grilled steak at 150 F., melon at 90 F., etc.
- **Welcome:** palatial.
- **Dress:** an attaché case.
- **Bottom line:** a Kissinger-style breakfast.
- **Cost:** 100 F., minimum.
- **Emergency alternative:** *Le George-V*, 31, avenue George-V, 8th. Tel.: 47.23.54.00. Cost: 85 F., including *madeleines*. An impeccable breakfast which has, unfortunately, become a victim of its success. The service can be unreasonably slow, and you're sure to run into someone you know.

# La Résidence du Bois ♥

## 9 a.m.

This place, listed in *Relais et Châteaux*, is more like a private home than a hotel . . . and a comfortably bourgeois one at that. It has been able to retain its secret charm, to the delight of its ever-faithful clientele. Having your morning coffee here is akin to visiting the home of a country doctor whose Napoleon III manor house boasts a slightly frayed Flemish tapestry, patched-up Louis XIII furniture, and a Boulle-style commode.

Lazily ensconced among the knickknacks in the salon, or relaxing in the inner court, it's hard to believe you're only a few steps away from the bustling place de l'Étoile.

- **With whom:** a close companion.
- **Where:** 16, rue Chalgrin, 16th. Tel.: 45.00.50.59. Between avenue Foch and the beginning of avenue de la Grande-Armée.
- **When:** every day from 8 a.m. Reservations advised.
- **Recommended:** the standard breakfast.
- **Welcome:** delightfully provincial.
- **Dress:** correct.
- **Bottom line:** a country breakfast.
- **Cost:** 80 F.
- **Emergency alternative:** The *Pub Winston Churchill*, 5, rue de Presbourg, 16th. Tel.: 45.00.75.35. Open from 9 a.m. If you don't mind a deserted place with shabby banquettes and half-awake waiters.

# Le Ritz ♥

*Place Vendôme*
Palatial

If you're staying at the Ritz, make sure to eat breakfast in the Espadon Salon, which features a veritable forest of green plants.

The famous courtesan "la belle Otero" would have loved stretching out in this winter garden on the curvaceous sofas, casting a blasé glance at the murals, fountains, arbors, and allegorical figures inspired by Versailles.

She wouldn't have deigned to look at the bankers, the fussy little ladies with their dogs, or the snow bunnies from Gstaad who now schuss into the Ritz; nor would she have grasped the incongruity of pompous, multilingual waiters in tails.

She would, though, adore the pastries made on the premises, and the scrambled eggs, but she would send back the soggy teabags and the frozen orange juice.

- **With whom:** a woman dear to your heart and your wallet.
- **Where:** 15, place Vendôme, 1st. Tel.: 42.60.38.30. Behind the line of limousines.
- **When:** every day from 7 to 11 a.m.
- **Recommended:** croissants and brioches, scrambled eggs extra.
- **Welcome:** admirable, of course, but aloof.
- **Dress:** up to snuff.
- **Bottom line:** pure unadulterated luxury, first thing in the morning.
- **Cost:** 115 F. for a meager breakfast, 150 F. for a real one.
- **Emergency alternative:** *Le Grand Hôtel*, 2, rue Scribe, 9th. Tel.: 42.68.12.13. The wonderful stained-glass window has disappeared, but the rich bankers are still there.

# Le Flore en l'Île   ♥

*10 a.m.*

♆

Le Flore en l'Île has gussied up its decor and cut back on its service. Regular customers will miss the casual friendliness of yesteryear, the informality of the waitresses, and the griminess of the bay windows. Now that it's become a proper spic-and-span tea room, the Flore seems more serious, but less appealing.

Fortunately, the loyal clientele doesn't seem to notice. The complete breakfast is still attractive, especially when it's topped off by some of Berthillon's famous chocolate ice cream. (Here, anything goes.) And somehow you'll keep returning, if only for the armchair view of Notre-Dame.

- **With whom:** late-rising residents from the Île Saint-Louis.
- **Where:** 42, quai d'Orléans, 4th. Tel.: 43.29.88.27. Opposite Notre-Dame.
- **When:** every day, from 10 a.m. to 1:45 a.m.
- **Recommended:** the complete breakfast (fresh orange juice, croissants and toast, soft-boiled eggs rather than fried), and perhaps some Berthillon ice cream.
- **Welcome:** now quite ordinary.
- **Dress:** disheveled.
- **Bottom line:** an eye-opening view.
- **Cost:** 60 F.
- **Emergency alternative:** *Sweet et Faim*, formerly *Annick Gendron* (which was nicer and less pretentious), 1, rue de la Bûcherie, 5th. Tel.: 43.25.82.16. From 9 a.m. to 2 a.m.

# Other Breakfast Suggestions

*Lo Stübli.* Ternes. 11, rue Poncelet, 17th. Tel.: 42.27.81.86. If you're bored by the pastoral pictures and botanical prints of this squeaky-clean place, if you're depressed by the dismally dowdy crowd at tea time, then come here for *breakfast*. Upstairs you'll find the best Viennese pastries in Paris, accompanied by a cup of hot chocolate with a dollop of cream that melts in your mouth. Closed Sunday. 40 F. ♆ ♆

*Les Domaines:* Étoile. 56, rue François-ler, 8th. Tel.: 42.56.15.87. For breakfast in the bright decorating style of Philippe Stark, try this fashionable wine bar. Depending on how hungry you are, choose the Parisian, British, or hearty country-style menu. Every day from 8 a.m. 50 F. ♆ ♆ ♆

*Le Dôme:* Montparnasse. 108, boulevard Montparnasse, 14th. Tel.: 43.35.25.81. On the serene terrace, forgotten by the waiters, you'll enjoy watching the first traffic jams of the day. Freshly brewed tea, slightly greasy toast. From 8 a.m. 40 F. La Coupole, just as empty at this hour, also serves breakfast, unlike Le Select and La Closerie which don't bother. ♆

*Le Terrass Hôtel:* Clichy. 12, rue Joseph-de-Maistre, 18th. Tel.: 46.06.72.85. For an abundant breakfast while sunning on the terrace. Service is slow, but as long as it's sunny you won't mind waiting. From 7 a.m. 65 F. ♆

*Café Costes:* Beaubourg. 4–6, rue Berger, 1st. Tel.: 45.08.54.39. Come to see the post-modern decor created by designer Christopher Cross (including wildly contemporary teapots), and (possibly) to taste the ham omelets. You can't depend on the croissants, and the waiters are ill-humored. It must be the early hour. ♆ ♆

# Le Lazy Brunch at the Hilton

**11 a.m.**

They've all stopped serving bountiful brunches: the Prince de Galles, the George-V, the Royal Monceau. The big hotels now prefer to serve a standard—and at times indifferent—breakfast every morning.

Fortunately, the Hilton maintains the brunch tradition and lets you feast in luxury after your morning jog or your Sunday concert at the Théâtre du Rond-Point, high up in the Toit de Paris restaurant facing the Eiffel Tower.

Smoked salmon is perhaps the only thing missing from this groaning board, which is laden with sparcribs, English sausages, and lightly caramelized bananas flambées.

- **With whom:** a big American-style eater.
- **Where:** 18, avenue de Suffren, 15th. Tel.: 42.73.92.00. Top floor, overlooking the soccer field.
- **When:** Sunday from 11:30 a.m. to 2:30 p.m.
- **Recommended:** the all-you-can-eat brunch menu.
- **Welcome:** à la Hilton International.
- **Dress:** a tie.
- **Bottom line:** the last surviving hotel brunch in Paris.
- **Cost:** 150 F.; 190 F. including a serving of roast meat.
- **Emergency alternative:** *Le Jazz Brunch* at the *Méridien* (p. 17).

# L'Ébouillanté ♥

## Noon

If you haven't been able to spend the weekend in the country, grab another forlorn city-dweller and console yourselves with brunch in a tiny house right next to the church of Saint-Gervais, on a cobbled, flowered street. You'll have to negotiate the narrow staircase, stoop under the low ceiling, squeeze into your chair, and search in vain for a place to fold your legs under the table. But, somehow, the discomfort only adds to the charm.

The attentive host will serve you his *bricks* (a kind of crisp, filled crêpe), *kefir* (like buttermilk, with mint), *taroudan* (like a milkshake), and tea from a samovar, to compensate for your being stuck in Paris. And your brunch rolls on and on. . . .

- **With whom:** an artist friend.
- **Where:** 6, rue de Barres, 4th. Tel.: 42.78.48.62. The cobbled street between the Louis-Philippe bridge and the church of Saint-Gervais.
- **When:** from noon to 9 p.m.; closed Monday.
- **Recommended:** the No. 2 brunch: corn flakes, soft-boiled eggs, stewed rhubarb. In addition, have some *bricks*, *tabbouleh*, Russian tea from the samovar, and—if you're unfamiliar with it—*kefir* and *taroudan*.
- **Not recommended:** the house pastries.
- **Welcome:** friendly.
- **Dress:** country style.
- **Bottom line:** for loafing about on Sunday.
- **Cost:** 70 F.
- **Emergency alternative:** *Le Flore en l'Île* (p. 13).

# Le Sunday Jazz Brunch at the Méridien

*Noon*

*Porte Maillot*
New York, New York

Is this pre-war New York, or postwar Paris?

The now paunchy, graying musicians of Claude Bolling's Big Band are wowing the audience from the podium. The Méridien's lobby is hardly big enough for the hundred or so tables that are crammed together and that are sold out three weeks in advance.

And it's no ordinary audience: show-biz personalities Jean Castel and Eddie Barclay, writer Gonzague Saint-Bris, TV newsman Yves Mourousi, along with the inevitable crowd of minor nobility and upper-class families, all greet each other solemnly over the smoked salmon, the rib roast, and the baked apples with brown sugar.

- **With whom:** daddy, mommy, and especially grandma.
- **Where:** 81, boulevard Gouvion-Saint-Cyr, 17th. Tel.: 47.58.12.30. In the lobby of the Hotel Méridien. Having reserved your table, good luck finding it.
- **When:** every Sunday from noon to 4 p.m., from October to April.
- **Recommended:** as much as you like; for once, plenty of salmon and high-quality meats.
- **Not recommended:** the pastries   very disappointing.
- **Welcome:** completely and understandably snowed under.
- **Dress:** remember you're at the epicenter of preppie territory.
- **Bottom line:** leave your visiting card on the buffet table.
- **Cost:** 230 F., including champagne and boogie-woogie.
- **Emergency alternative:** during the summer, you'll find the same crowd for brunch at *L'Espace* (p. 21).

# Le Swimming Brunch at the Royal-Monceau ♥

*Noon*

Roman decadence has its charm. Brunching to music beside a sumptuous pool is enough to make you forget the rigors of Parisian life.

From the moment you enter, you might as well be in Pompeii: stucco and Mediterranean frescoes everywhere (including one of Venus at her bath). Lutèce lives again in this luxurious spa complete with atrium and surrounded by marble statues, columns, and galleries.

But the spirit of the place is more dietetic than decadent, so don't be surprised when your Tahitian hostess prepares you a wonderful dish of raw fish marinated in lime. (Gourmands can gleefully devour the pastries and the poached eggs, or even treat themselves to caviar.)

Be careful not to get splashed by overzealous swimmers!

- **With whom:** a statuesque beauty, like Esther Williams.
- **Where:** 39, avenue Hoche, 8th. Tel.: 42.25.06.66. Separate entrance, alongside the Hôtel Royal-Monceau.
- **When:** the swimming brunch is served every day from noon to 3:30 p.m., on Sunday from 10 a.m. to 6 p.m.
- **Recommended:** the Tahitian brunch, but ten other choices are available.
- **Welcome:** delightful, flowers and all.
- **Dress:** have a swimsuit handy, in case you succumb.
- **Bottom line:** a fitness brunch.
- **Cost:** 150 F. for brunch, and 350 F. to use the thermal baths.

- ○ **Emergency alternative:** the buffet breakfast at the Hôtel Royal-Monceau, served just one flight up in the winter garden. Guaranteed to have a business-like ambience.

# Chez Guy ♥

## 1 p.m.

Party it up some Saturday. Granted, for some people it's a day of rest or a day of boredom, but at Chez Guy, as in Rio, it's the day for *feijoada.*

This Brazilian cassoulet, loaded with black beans, sausage, and rice, may seem heavy to you, but it's lightened with manioc flour, greens, and oranges, and most important, it's washed down with plenty of *batida,* a lemony punch.

After the feast, Cléa sings and gradually the rhythm of the samba will overtake you, just as it did in *Black Orpheus.* You'll finally throw caution to the wind and dance—on the tables, winding in and out of the orchestra, everywhere.

Afterward you'll want to take a well-earned nap in that tempting hammock, which seems to be beckoning already.

- **With whom:** some *bons vivants,* or a budding Carmen.
- **Where:** 6, rue Mabillon, 6th. Tel.: 43.54.87.61. Opposite the "restau U" (a student canteen); hard to see from the street.
- **When:** brunch on Saturday only; come at 12:30 p.m. and stay as long as you like. Also open every evening except Sunday from 8 p.m. to 1 a.m.
- **Recommended** (and compulsory): *batida, feijoada,* and *quindim* (little coconut cakes).
- **Welcome:** fraternal.
- **Dress:** designer jeans.
- **Bottom line:** like a Brazilian festival.
- **Cost:** 165 F.
- **Emergency alternative:** *Macadam,* 1, rue Delambre, 14th. Tel.: 43.35.43.86. Sunday brunch from 11:30 a.m. to 4 p.m. 70 F.

# Other Brunches, Other Styles

*Magnetic Terrace:* 12, rue de la Cossonerie, 1st. Tel.: 42.36.26.44. Sunday from noon to 4 p.m. For 115 F., a bountiful buffet: fruit salad, cereal, scrambled eggs with tarragon. Artists, models, assorted pretentious types — very much in the style of the Forum des Halles, with a video screen to boot.

*L'Espace:* 1, avenue Gabriel, 8th. Tel.: 42.66.11.70. Sunday from noon to 4 p.m. Very show-biz and light-hearted. Worth going for the garden and just to line up behind French celebrities at the buffet table. But where on earth are the pancakes?
Also: *L'Aviatic* (p. 180) and *Le Café Pacifico* (p. 183).

## For Conversation

*Le Quatrième sans Ascenseur:* 8, rue des Écouffes, 4th. Tel.: 48.87.39.26. Sunday from noon to 4 p.m. A delicious brunch for 93 F.: eggs scrambled with lots of different ingredients, toast and marmalade, freshly squeezed fruit juices, tea or coffee. A quiet room and gracious service for conservative folks. But the waiters do seem to resent working on Sunday.

*Art et Buffet:* 16, rue de la Grand-Chaumière, 6th. Tel.: 46.34.24.16. Sunday from 11 a.m. to 6 p.m. A meager brunch for 75 F. Tasteless coffee. A neat studio for an artsy clientele, right near Montparnasse. Closed July and August.

## For Lazing About

*Pandora:* 24, passage Choiseul, 2nd. Tel.: 42.97. 56.01. From noon to 7 p.m. A cozy salon in a sleepy passageway. Brunch consists of fresh fruit juice, toast, scrambled eggs, soft white cheese, and pancakes — plus a smile — all for 98 F. Closed Saturday.

*Thé Cool:* 10, rue Jean-Bologne, 16th. Tel.: 42.24.69.13. Facing the church of Passy. From 11 a.m.

to 6 p.m., a hearty brunch for 50 to 120 F. Also recommended: the *marquise au chocolat*. A sweet, unaffected welcome and comfortable armchairs to help you forget it's a dull Sunday in Passy.

*Les Jardins de la Paresse:* Parc Montsouris. 20, rue Gazan, 14th. Tel.: 45.88.38.52. Brunch served only until noon. After that, you have to order lunch. Mountain-cured ham, cucumbers with mint, scrambled eggs, fruit juices. So much for the brunch . . . but what a delightful ambience!
Also: the brunch menus at *Carr's* (p. 111) and especially at *Olsson's* (p. 155), where the trend is toward yogurt, muesli, and eggs Benedict (75 F.).

## U.S. Come Home

Utterly essential: Bloody Mary, pancakes, and scrambled eggs. 65 F. (starting at noon).

*Mother Earth:* 66, rue des Lombards, 1st. Tel.: 42.36.35.58. The brunch here still attracts loyal customers, but it's on the way out. Too heavy.

*Le Diable des Lombards:* 64, rue des Lombards, 1st. Tel.: 42.33.81.84. No character, but it's picking up customers from its neighbor, Mother Earth.

*Conway's:* 73, rue Saint-Denis, 1st. Tel.: 45.08.07.70. The gloomiest place, but also the most intimate if you happen to be seated in a booth.

And finally, for California Chic, *Le Café Pacifico* (p. 183).

# Noon

*Lunch with Friends*
*Business Lunches*
*Lunch on-the-run*

# L'Artois

L'Artois is the name of the street. The Baie des Anges, pictured over the bar, is just for decoration. The seal of Auvergne, which hides the coat-of-arms of the Count d'Artois over the mantelpiece, represents the region. But Raymond Rouzeyrol, the owner, is actually from Corrèze, and proud of it.

Whenever his health permitted, he would come in and join the fans watching the soccer matches. The hefty wine steward often had to break up a number of scrimmages around the bar.

These days, the noisy crowd comes to enjoy the good food and have a few bottles of Cahors. The *fritons* are light; the *rillettes* and terrines melt in your mouth, and healthy portions are served; and, in season, the roast rabbit with fresh *cèpes* gives you a good grip on life. The Cantal cheese comes straight from Salers, and after dessert (a parfait or a *religieuse*—coffee- or chocolate-coated choux pastry puffs in the shape of a nun), you simply can't refuse a glass of armagnac, which is usually on the house.

- **With whom:** some Corréziens, so you're sure to be offered the armagnac.
- **Where:** 13, rue d'Artois, 8th. Tel.: 42.25.01.10. At the corner of rue Frédéric-Bastiat, near Saint-Philippe-du-Roule.
- **When:** from noon to 3 p.m. and 7:15 to 9:30 p.m.; closed Saturday and Sunday.
- **Recommended:** *fritons* or terrine, *coq au vin*, tripe or *boeuf bourguignon*, *religieuses* with *café liégeois*. Accompanied by a Cahors.
- **Not recommended:** the partridge.
- **Welcome:** like in the provinces.
- **Dress:** formal.
- **Bottom line:** a festive little feast among friends.

- **Cost:** 200 F.
- **Emergency alternative:** *Chez Germain*, 19, rue Mermoz, 8th. Tel.: 43.59.29.24. Packed and friendly.

# Aux Négociants

*Noon*

The oldtimers at the Négociants bar, a stubborn breed with thick moustaches, have never understood the stampede of young customers who are all in a hurry to gulp down the *plat du jour* with a quick glass of wine. The young journalists from *Libé*, in fact, come here especially for "le quick snack."

The owner couldn't care less, ensconced behind his horseshoe-shaped bar, avidly thumbing through his farm magazines, while his faithful old waiter runs from table to table, setting down his terrines and refilling empty glasses with Brouilly, Chenas, or Gris Meunier.

A heavy hook on the ceiling marks the entrance to the wine cellar. What a privilege it would be to venture down there!

- **With whom:** a really good drinker.
- **Where:** 27, rue Lambert, 18th. Tel.: 46.06.15.11. Follow rue Custine, which begins at boulevard Barbès (Métro station Château-Rouge).
- **When:** from 11:30 a.m. to 9 p.m., on Tuesday and Thursday until 10 p.m.; closed Saturday and Sunday.
- **Recommended:** excellent *hure* (head cheese) with pistachios, the *plat du jour*, strong livarot cheese, noteworthy lesser wines from the Loire.
- **Welcome:** hurried.
- **Dress:** anything ordinary.
- **Bottom line:** a picturesque old bistrot on the Butte de Montmartre.
- **Cost:** less than 5 F. for a glass of wine, 80 F. for everything.
- **Emergency alternative:** *La Maison Rose* (p. 34).

# Cercle Musicale
# Rachmaninov ♥

## Noon

Chaillot
Mother Russia

Slightly tatty, the canteen of the Cercle Musicale Rachmaninov—located in the cellar of a private town house—doesn't even try to keep up appearances anymore. Oilcloth, tiles, simple wood chairs, and cheap wallpaper: it's hard to maintain your image when you're an impoverished White Russian!

There are ancestral portraits over the fireplace and paintings of the Taiga, which remind nostalgic visitors and music lovers of their homeland while they relish some of the best Russian cooking in Paris.

Be respectful, please, to the professors (who sit at their own reserved table) and to the bearded old Russians with faraway looks, picking at their malassol caviar.

Warm-hearted, motherly waitresses fawn over them, but don't be afraid to interrupt. When all is said and done, the Russian Circle is a family circle.

- **With whom:** snobs, music lovers, or dethroned princes.
- **Where:** 26, avenue de New-York, 16th. Tel.: 47.20.65.17. Between the Palais de Tokyo and the Trocadéro.
- **When:** from noon to 2 p.m. and 7:15 to 9:30 p.m.; closed Sunday, and Monday at noon.
- **Recommended:** borscht, roast piglet with kasha, *vatrouchka* (a cheesecake), Zoubrovska vodka; blinis with smoked salmon in the evening.
- **Welcome:** sometimes brusque, but friendly.
- **Dress:** patched together.
- **Bottom line:** to feel like a real White Russian.
- **Cost:** 80 F. for the annual membership card which you purchase there. Less than 100 F. for a meal.
- **Emergency alternative:** *Le Bar des Théâtres* (p. 67).

# Les Cinq Points Cardinaux

*Noon*

The passage Saint-Bernard could have been the inspiration for the setting of a Truffaut film: boarded-up hardware, plumbing, and electricity stores; a prostitute's calling card stuck on a door; and a few vacant lots where some neighborhood kids play ball.

One of those kids probably scrawled on the window of this grocery store/restaurant: "You eat cheap here, no foolin'—whether you're a lady or a tramp, brawny or brainy."

And it's true: artists and craftsmen, construction workers and journalists, squeeze in here unceremoniously, under the old shears, blowtorches, clamps, and other outdated tools. The scene resembles a composition by Fernand Léger.

- **With whom:** some footloose buddies.
- **Where:** 7, passage Saint-Bernard, 11th. Tel.: 47.00.89.00. A paved passageway that starts under a portal opposite 159, faubourg Saint-Antoine.
- **When:** from noon to 3 p.m. for lunch; closed Saturday and Sunday.
- **Recommended:** *rillettes*, rabbit stew, or "steak P.V." (steak with steamed potatoes), semolina cake with frangipani.
- **Welcome:** as attractive as the owner's daughter.
- **Dress:** blue overalls.
- **Bottom line:** a quick lunch break.
- **Cost:** 41.50 F.
- **Emergency alternative:** *Chez Paul* (p. 35).

# Du Côté de l'Arsenal

## Noon

On a forgotten quay along the Saint-Martin canal, far from the paths, the locks, and the warehouses of the Quai de Jemmapes, these three bistros seem strangely familiar: could it be vacation memories, films about the Front Populaire, or Simenon novels?

Trucks are parked in front, houseboats are moored a little farther on, and both groups—travelers and dockers—have the chance to get together over a meal.

*Au Rendez-vous de la Marine:* 14, quai de la Loire, 19th. Tel.: 42.49.33.40. Closed Saturday, Sunday, and Monday. Come between noon and 2 p.m. The owner and the chef, both of them plump and pleasant, are a living tribute to their homemade *pâté de tête* and *confit maison.* An easy-going ambience. 80 F.

*Au Rendez-vous du Port:* the same kind of place, but quieter, at no. 20 on the same quai. Tel.: 42.05.90.53. The ruddy-faced owner sports a crew-cut and a pencil behind his ear. You can lunch on a plateful of pasta for 6 F., but you have to pay 50 centimes extra for grated cheese. Things are tough all over. Closed Sunday.

*Au Bon Accueil de Seine-et-Marne:* 86, quai de la Loire, 19th. Tel.: 42.05.01.37. Closed Saturday and Sunday between noon and 1 p.m. Cheerful Mademoiselle Raymonde can down her wine, flip the crêpes, and monopolize the conversation with all the latest gossip, all at the same time. For 50 F., what could be better? But to be admitted, you have to have a certain "look."

# L'Entracte

## Noon

This "entracte," far more than the "intermission" at the neighboring Palais-Royal, is a spectacle in itself—as fluffy as a Feydeau farce. On the terrace, the characters in this comedy look like wax figures. Above the bar, a two-cornered hat and a helmet have been tossed among the banknotes tacked to the ceiling.

You'll lunch in a wine cellar decorated to look like a Provençal garden, with a bower of flowers, parasol pines, plumed reeds, and even a Parisian streetlight on which some joker has hung a few trout.

The curtain has fallen on the wonderful duo who ran this comic place. The new owners seem full of promise. Let's hope it lasts.

- o **With whom:** a Supreme Court judge, far from his colleagues.
- o **Where:** 4, rue Montpensier, 1st. Tel.: 42.97.57.76. Opposite the Palais-Royal Theater, in the bend of the street.
- o **When:** from noon to 3 p.m. and 6 p.m. to 2 a.m.; dinner served only until 11 p.m.; closed Monday.
- o **Recommended:** just one dish: *gratin de jambonneau* (ham gratinée) or *feuilleté au fromage/jambon* (flaky pastry filled with cheese or ham); Lirac by the glass.
- o **Not recommended:** the commercially made pastries.
- o **Welcome:** friendly.
- o **Dress:** a straw boater, like Maurice Chevalier.
- o **Bottom line:** lunch under the bower.
- o **Cost:** 80 F.
- o **Emergency alternative:** *La Gaudriole*, 30, rue Montpensier, 1st. Tel.: 42.97.55.49. Only enjoyable during the summer, because of the terrace on the Palais-Royal side. The waiters are snowed under, and the menu at 130 F. is forgettable.

# L'Entre Deux Verres   ♥

*Noon*

If you love châteaux and bordeaux, you'll be greeted with open arms at L'Entre Deux Verres.

True, the rue Sainte-Anne looks like a risky street, but you'll find that it's quite safe at noon. The courtyard, too, may look dilapidated: you wouldn't want to poke around here without some reassurances. And the restaurant doesn't even have a sign on the street: its reputation is enough to keep it packed.

Old school chums, respectable young bankers, subscribers to the Comédie Française—they all get along well in this 17th-century wine cellar, where the ambience is as prim and proper as a landmarks preservation meeting.

The cooking reflects an enlightened amateurism. The wines are selected with savoir-faire, and to head off mistakes, an aptly named "accompanying" menu is suggested for each one.

- **With whom:** someone you've just met.
- **Where:** 48, rue Sainte-Anne, 2nd. Tel.: 42.96.42.26. Next to the rue des Petits-Champs, at the back of the courtyard, on the right-hand side.
- **When:** from noon to 3 p.m.; closed Saturday and Sunday.
- **Recommended:** the "Entre Deux-Mers" menu: *quenelles de brochet*, cheese platter, and a glass of Peyrines; also the *gâteau glacé*, which costs extra.
- **Welcome:** hospitable.
- **Dress:** preppie.
- **Bottom line:** on the run, in good company.
- **Cost:** 100 F.
- **Emergency alternative:** *Pandora* (pp. 21, 97).

# Jacques Melac

## Noon

Far East
Spontaneous

Parts of Paris resemble a village. This wine bistro, for example, in the heart of a deserted neighborhood that has been demolished and carelessly rebuilt, just between the boulevard Voltaire and the Père-Lachaise cemetery, is as low key as it would be were it in Ardèche.

And in fact, the moustachioed owner wearing a checked shirt is really from that region. He extends a warm welcome to his cronies and the neighborhood kids, and discusses the coming harvest with deep concern. (There's a vineyard outside his restaurant.)

In this comfortable crush, under the sausages suspended from the ceiling, dig into the Cantal omelets, the Auvergne cheeses, and the fruit *flognardes* (cakelike tarts), and wash it all down generously with some "little" wine, sold by the glass or *au compteur* (from the bottle).

- **With whom:** some cheerful chums.
- **Where:** 42, rue Léon-Frot, 11th. Tel.: 43.70.59.27. From the Bastille, down rue Charonne, the second street on the right after boulevard Voltaire.
- **When:** from noon to 7 p.m.; closed Sunday and Monday. Late nights on Tuesday and Thursday. Don't miss the harvest in September.
- **Recommended:** the *plat du jour* or the Cantal omelet; cheese platter; then you'll have no room for dessert.
- **Not recommended:** the apple *clafoutis* (fruit flan); water (held in low esteem).
- **Welcome:** heart-warming.
- **Dress:** rolled-up sleeves.
- **Bottom line:** at last—a real wine bistro!
- **Cost:** 80 F.; a glass of wine is 4.80 F.
- **Emergency alternative:** *À Sousceyrac*, 35, rue

Faidherbe, 11th. Tel.: 43.71.65.30. A price notch above (280 F.) for marvelous sweetbreads and a matchless plum liqueur. Closed Saturday and Sunday.

# La Maison Rose

*Noon*

Montmartre
Straightforward

Long before Utrillo painted it, the vine-covered Maison Rose was a well-known inn outside the city to which Parisians flocked for a relaxing drink.

Now very staid, with its pink plaster walls, this sentimental place welcomes residents of the Butte and a few wandering tourists. The ambience is rather southern, the service Mediterranean, the cuisine plentiful and straightforward: big salads, very good steaks, light flaky *feuilletés* of fish, and tasty pies.

One criticism: the music is too loud. And why don't they play Trenet or Piaf (whose photos hang on the wall)?

- **With whom:** ordinary tourists or bucolic Parisians.
- **Where:** 2, rue de l'Abreuvoir, 18th. Tel.: 42.64.54.64. North side of the Butte, next to the Montmartre vineyard.
- **When:** from noon to 2:30 p.m. and 7 to 11 p.m.; closed Monday at noon. Nicer at lunchtime (for the view) and in the summer (on the terrace).
- **Recommended:** *aiguillettes de canard* (long thin slices of duck) *aux petits oignons confits*, pie; the house wine.
- **Not recommended:** the salad with chèvre cheese (unmelted).
- **Welcome:** smiling and sunny.
- **Dress:** in Montmartre, you're in the country.
- **Bottom line:** blissfully lazy.
- **Cost:** 100 F. maximum.
- **Emergency alternative:** at noon, *Au Tournant de la Butte*, 46, rue Caulaincourt, 18th. Tel.: 42.51.74.96. Evening: *Au Virage Lepic*, 61, rue Lepic, 18th. Tel.: 42.52.46.79. For real Montmartre dinners.

**34** LUNCH WITH FRIENDS

# Chez Paul

Bastille
Rough and ready

Monsieur Paul, from Aveyron, operates on the same principles as his neighbor, Henri Queuille from Corrèze: to survive for a long time, do nothing. Don't clean up the blackened mirrors or the old hotplate, don't improve the comfort of the grungy room which is practically part of the kitchen, and do continue to spread sawdust on the floor.

Well, business is business. There's a lot of joking around with the customers—craftsmen from the faubourg Saint-Antoine and journalists from *Actuel*—while prodding them to order more: "Take a whole bottle. With half a bottle, you'll only have one and a half glassfuls."

Then, the joking stops and Monsieur Paul adds up the bill.

But you've had a great meal: the snails were tasty, the crudités came fresh from the market, and the pies were really country style.

- **With whom:** some good pals, some journalists.
- **Where:** 13, rue de Charonne, 11th. Tel.: 47.00.34.57. At the end of the rue de Lappe.
- **When:** from noon to 3 p.m. and 7:30 to 9 p.m.; closed Saturday and Sunday. Livelier at lunchtime.
- **Recommended:** snails or crudités, beef bourguignon or steak tartare, orange tart, beaujolais wine.
- **Not recommended:** the apple tart.
- **Welcome:** too rustic to be real.
- **Dress:** rugged.
- **Bottom line:** decidedly going back to your roots.
- **Cost:** 120 F.
- **Emergency alternative:** *Restaurant Antoine*, 7, rue Saint-Nicolas, 12th. Tel.: 43.43.49.40. Tie a napkin around your neck and dig in: cold cuts, *bôeuf gros sel* (boiled beef with coarse sea salt), and a thick pear tart. Breathtaking. 170 F., which includes the whole merry scene.

# Polidor

## Noon

The years have been kind to the Crèmerie Restaurant Polidor. The old furniture and the etched-glass windows are still there. The backroom, where the oldtimers go, sparkles with colorful frescoes in the Poiret style. As for the toilets—they overlook the Philippe Auguste wall.

If the Polidor could speak, it would tell us tales about Verlaine and Rimbaud, about the literary battles of the 1930s, and about Léautaud's quarrels and his 36 cats.

Nothing has changed since then, not even the menu. The pumpkin soup tastes like mother's very own, the kidneys in cream are prepared according to an age-old recipe, the applesauce is made from apples grown in the garden, and the coffee is slowly filtered through an antique apparatus.

Polidor is irreplaceable.

- **With whom:** an established author or a struggling poet.
- **Where:** 41, rue Monsieur-le-Prince, 6th. Tel.: 43.26.95.34. Next to the Odéon Theater.
- **When:** from noon to 2:30 p.m. and 7 to 10 p.m.; closed Sunday and Monday.
- **Recommended:** cream of pumpkin soup or Bourgogne snails, kidneys *à la crème* or rabbit with mustard, tarte Tatin or baba au rhum, filtered coffee; Saint-Amour wine.
- **Welcome:** motherly.
- **Dress:** like a life-long student.
- **Bottom line:** long live the Latin Quarter!
- **Cost:** 80 F.
- **Emergency alternative:** *Les Cinq Points Cardinaux* (p. 28).

# La Reine Margot

Plans to modernize this place really had me worried, but fortunately, even though it has changed, La Reine Margot has kept the discreet charm of the 7th arrondissement: old family mementos, an astonishing ability to create fresh and different daily specials, and a strong sense of value.

So it's just like old times for the regular customers, including a few government ministers on a spree, some diplomats going off the beaten track, and young executives who like the bustling graciousness of the owner. In summer, the best places are on the terrace, where you can gaze at the Invalides and eavesdrop, of course, on your neighbors.

- **With whom:** not with anyone from work; they'll disturb the peace.
- **Where:** 36, rue Fabert, 7th. Tel.: 45.51.26.98. Right on the esplanade of the Invalides, near the rue de l'Université.
- **When:** from noon to 3 p.m. and 8 to 11 p.m.; closed Saturday evening and all day Sunday.
- **Recommended:** the *plats du jour*, for example: salmon *rillettes*, mixed brochette, and pies (according to the season).
- **Not recommended:** the Williams salad.
- **Welcome:** from the bottom of the heart.
- **Dress:** inconspicuous.
- **Bottom line:** homey.
- **Cost:** 100 F.
- **Emergency alternative:** *Le Sancerre*, 22, avenue Rapp, 7th. Tel.: 45.51.75.91. Closed Saturday evening and all day Sunday. Just a hop away from the television studios of Cognacq-Jay, so it's fun to go slumming with the famous. Warning: the *andouillette* (sausage made with chitterlings) washed down with a glass of Sancerre at lunchtime is bound to make you drowsy.

# Au Rendez-vous des Camionneurs

## Noon

Judges from the Supreme Court of Appeal, police commissioners, and homosexual couples seem to share similar tastes: they all go to the Rendez-vous des Camionneurs . . . at different times, of course.

At noon, Madame Jacqueline is honored by the distinguished presence of Law and Order, and in the evening, she's deeply moved by the friendliness of her gay community, among whom you'll find the tough leather crowd and maybe a few truckers.

Assisted by a typical street-smart Parisian, she smiles as she serves up family-style country cuisine featuring leeks vinaigrette, *petit salé* (ham hock) with lentils, and rice cake. Out of respect for her customers, she adds up the check very carefully, to the last centime, and suggests that you keep your napkin for the next visit.

- **With whom:** a judge at noon, a gay blade in the evening.
- **Where:** 72, quai des Orfèvres, 1st. Tel.: 43.54.88.74. A stone's throw from the statue of Henri IV.
- **When:** from noon to 2:30 p.m. and 8 to 11 p.m. Totally different by day and by night. It's a good idea to reserve.
- **Recommended:** celery *rémoulade* or leeks vinaigrette, *petit salé* (ham hock) with lentils, rice cake or *clafoutis* (fruit flan).
- **Not recommended:** the pâté, the *andouillette*, the lemon pie.
- **Welcome:** like one big family.
- **Dress:** don't overdo it.
- **Bottom line:** a big-hearted bistro.

- **Cost:** 80 F.
- **Emergency alternative:** *Le Caveau du Palais,* 19 place Dauphine, 1st. Tel.: 43.26.04.28. You might see Yves Montand, who lives nearby.

# Le Rubis

## Noon

Saint-Honoré
Serious

At lunch there's a throng of neighborhood merchants, sports enthusiasts, and bankers from Paribas clustered around the bar, eagerly quaffing great wines from Beaujolais and "little" wines from Bordeaux, perhaps accompanied by some ham *persillé* or some roquefort cheese.

Tucked away upstairs, the restaurant is calmer, like the backroom of a provincial roadside inn. The waitress, grumbling or joking depending on her mood, will announce the *plats du jour*.

Don't even think about talking business. Instead, take advantage of the chance to listen in on your neighbors at the next table.

- **With whom:** a friendly business associate.
- **Where:** 10, rue du Marché-Saint-Honoré, 1st. Tel.: 42.61.03.34. Between the rue Saint-Honoré and the firehouse.
- **When:** from 6:45 a.m. to 10 p.m. Closed Saturday and Sunday.
- **Recommended:** the ham *persillé*, lamb sauté or warm sausage, pear flan; Morgon or Graves wine. A different *plat du jour* every day.
- **Not recommended:** the strawberry pie.
- **Welcome:** warm.
- **Dress:** anything from work clothes to a three-piece suit.
- **Bottom line:** the Beaujolais pause that refreshes.
- **Cost:** 80 F.
- **Emergency alternative:** *Le Dauphin*, 167, rue Saint-Honoré, 1st. Tel.: 42.60.40.11. A fixed menu at 53.50 F.

# Le Trumilou

Hôtel-de-Ville
Regional

Artisans appreciate work well done, so those in the neighborhood have gladly adopted Le Trumilou. And indeed the restaurant deserves their recognition.

The portions are huge enough to appease any workingman's appetite. The decoration is ordinary, with wild boar heads (the carcass most likely went into a stew) hung alongside bucolic scenes (probably donated by starving artists as payment for their meals).

Neophytes will order the menu at 50 F., but experienced hands will take the one at 65 F., replacing the crudités with salad Niçoise, the sautéed chicken with sautéed lamb, the camembert with Cantal, and the crème caramel with the excellent coffee ice cream.

Then they'll pay their respects to the owner, standing behind the bar, and his wife, operating the cash register. Both are in their working smocks, proud and gruff— like Gabin and Signoret in the movies—earnestly running their establishment.

- **With whom:** buddies from the army.
- **Where:** 84, quai de l'Hôtel-de-Ville, 4th. Tel.: 42.77.63.98. Between the Pont d'Arcole and the Pont Louis-Philippe. The terrace is not advised; the private room is nice.
- **When:** from noon to 2 p.m. and 7 to 8 p.m.; closed Monday.
- **Recommended:** salad Niçoise, lamb sauté, Cantal cheese, coffee ice cream.
- **Welcome:** rustic.
- **Dress:** anything; a napkin around your neck is okay.
- **Bottom line:** a very homey place.
- **Cost:** under 80 F.
- **Emergency alternative:** *Brasserie du Pont-Louis-Philippe*, 66 quai de l'Hôtel-de-Ville, 4th. Tel.: 42.72.29.42.

# Les Salons Weber   ♥

*Buttes-Chaumont*
Open-air

Struggling artists and lost souls on the Buttes-Chaumont? Don't believe it—it's just part of the legend. You have only to look at the contented families out for a Sunday stroll, or the determined joggers puffing over hill and dale. . . .

Les Salons Weber reflect this simple, stable life. The management has kept the stodgy old name, has never called in a decorator, and doesn't get upset over discussions of *nouvelle cuisine.*

On the other hand, the wallpaper makes it look cozy, the carefully framed Renoir reproductions suggest a taste for tradition, and the regional specialties (as well as the selection of cheese) are above reproach.

But do excuse the cook, who is sometimes too ambitious, and the waiter, who is constantly calling his boss for help. Enjoy the well-heeled clientele, who live off their investments and their real estate, and take advantage of one of the prettiest terraces in Paris.

- o **With whom:** the whole family.
- o **Where:** avenue de la Cascade, in the Buttes-Chaumont park, 19th. Tel.: 46.07.58.14. Southeast of the Buttes, on the side of rue de Crimée.
- o **When:** from noon to 3 p.m. Lunch only. Closed Monday.
- o **Recommended:** the tarte Tatin.
- o **Welcome:** pleasant.
- o **Dress:** Sunday best.
- o **Bottom line:** dependable; lovely terrace in the summer.
- o **Cost:** 120 F.
- o **Emergency alternative:** the classier *Pavillon du Lac,* also in the park. Tel.: 42.02.08.97. 250 F.

# Le Bristol  ♥

## 1 p.m.

The British still go to the Bristol. After all, being next to the Élysée Palace can lead to some interesting encounters, and being near the faubourg Saint-Honoré and avenue Matignon makes for easy shopping. Besides, it's the best hotel restaurant in town, isn't it?

True enough, these spacious and stylish rooms exude a British kind of serenity. In winter, the gentlemen like to lunch in this Louis XV candybox, hung with Flemish tapestries, lit by crystal fixtures, and enlivened by symbolic frescoes. In summer, the room is turned into a military tent, with fabric covering the walls.

Alas, it will be hard for you to concentrate on business. This sort of setting makes you think less about cash flow than about posies in the garden. *Tant pis.*

- **With whom:** Germans and Englishmen, who adore the hotel.
- **Where:** 112, rue du Faubourg Saint-Honoré, 8th. Tel.: 42.66.91.45. Between the Élysée Palace and avenue Matignon.
- **When:** from 12:30 to 2 p.m. and 8 to 10:30 p.m. Lunch is preferable, so you can see the garden in daylight.
- **Recommended:** *tartare* of salmon and oysters, *escalope* of turbot with sauterne, *gratin* of fresh fruit or apple charlotte. A crazy wine list. Choose a Saumur Champigny or a Blanc de Blanc Salon Le Mesnil.
- **Welcome:** palatial.
- **Dress:** à la faubourg Saint-Honoré.
- **Bottom line:** for a smashing business lunch or a full-dress lovers' lunch.
- **Cost:** 450 F.
- **Emergency alternative:** *Hôtel de Crillon* (p. 9). In the winter, the Salon des Ambassadeurs; in the summer, the courtyard.

# La Denise Fabre
# Connection

## 1 p.m.

*Hyped-up*

Two places where you'll enjoy having business lunches: both very Parisian with a deceptively rustic air, both run by the ever-smiling Denise Fabre (a top television announcer) and her husband (a creative chef).

*Le Manoir de Paris:* ideal for a public relations-style lunch in the Ternes area. The old Grand Veneur, now the Manoir de Paris, has a Manneristic decor: Tiffany ceiling, photomontages by Arcimboldo, a menu so fancy it's illegible, and an affected way of serving that rattles too many metal dishcovers. But your client will be overwhelmed by the Japanese-inspired delicacy of the award-winning cuisine, and will be enchanted by the chic Parisian clientele. *Noix de Saint-Jacques à la mode de Gevrey* (scallops Gevrey style), *suprême de barbue* (filet of brill), *cassis opéra* (cassis-flavored Bavarian cream).

6, rue Pierre-Demours, 17th. Tel.: 45.72.25.25. From noon to 2 p.m. and 7 to 10:15 p.m.; closed Saturday and Sunday. 400 F.

*La Ferme Saint-Simon:* for a relaxed business lunch in the Saint-Germain area. The decor is sober yet airy, and both rooms are very countrified, making this a good, unpretentious place to bring high-placed local officials. The menu of the day at 178 F. (wine and service included) won't look extravagant on your expense account. Noteworthy: a succulent raspberry/pistachio marzipan, and profiteroles with mint.

6, rue Saint-Simon, 7th. Tel.: 45.48.35.74. From noon to 10:30 p.m.; closed Saturday at noon and all day Sunday.

# Le Divellec

**1 p.m.**

*Invalides*
Maritime

The prospect of having a business lunch right next to the Invalides isn't very appealing. Restaurants like La Flamberge and La Bourgogne are laughably pretentious, Le Quai d'Orsay is too packed to allow for the exchange of any real confidences, and Chez les Anges can serve such a heavy lunch that you're unable to work for the rest of the afternoon.

Thank heavens for Le Divellec. It's like a breath of brisk sea air, and offers fresh fish, seafood, and even eels (wriggling about in a fishtank before they end up in a stew).

In this cool and airy setting, surrounded by bright seascape paintings, you're in for a delightful surprise: the business lunch crowd is mostly women.

- **With whom:** a businesswoman.
- **Where:** 107, rue de l'Université, 7th. Tel.: 45.51.91.96. On the esplanade of the Invalides.
- **When:** from 12:30 to 2:30 p.m. and 8 to 10 p.m.; closed Sunday and Monday.
- **Recommended:** the fixed menu, of course, but also the *langoustines* with *foie gras*, and the fresh pasta with squid ink.
- **Welcome:** relaxed.
- **Dress:** a navy-blue suit.
- **Bottom line:** a little bit like a vacation.
- **Cost:** 400 F. At noon, a copious fixed menu at 220 F.
- **Emergency alternative:** cross over the Seine.

# Chez Edgard

I won't mince words: Edgard has become—especially at lunchtime—the Brasserie Lipp of the Right Bank. Government ministers who've been interviewed on television, deputies making important contacts, journalists stalking a scoop—all the movers and shakers of Parisian life mingle here.

Monsieur Paul skillfully arranges his star-studded cast, his inimitable waitresses cluck like mother hens, and the cloakroom lady—irresistibly street-wise—won't tolerate any nonsense.

The rich and famous hole up in the private salons, members of the fourth estate hang out in the glass-enclosed booths, and nobody knows who is hatching what under the staircase, in the nooks reserved for shady characters.

- **With whom:** choose him/her carefully—you're being watched.

- **Where:** 4, rue Marbeuf, 8th. Tel. 47.20.51.15. Almost at avenue George-V.

- **When:** from noon to 2:30 p.m. and 8 p.m. to 12:30 a.m.; closed Sunday.

- **Recommended:** oysters, salmon *tartare*, mousse au chocolat.

- **Not recommended:** *gratin* of lotte (burbot) with fresh noodles, coffee-flavored *brésilienne* for dessert.

- **Welcome:** get adopted by a waitress, such as Marie-Claude, if you're lucky.

- **Dress:** prosperous.

- **Bottom line:** VIP lunches.

- **Cost:** 250 F.

- **Emergency alternative:** *Chez André*, 12, Rue Marbeuf, 8th. Tel.: 47.20.59.57. Nothing has changed here, either: some of the waiters have been here close to 35 years, the gladiolas are always fresh, the *gigot* of lamb with mashed potatoes is first-class. But tourists are starting to get to know the place. Closed Tuesday.

# Extension 13

## 1 p.m.

The canteen of filmmaker Claude Lelouch is well guarded. Do you dare sneak into Studio 13, stride nonchalantly past the cloakroom attendant, and make a bee-line for the screening room?

Leatherette armchairs, low coffee tables, and pine paneling add to the clubby atmosphere of Lelouch's domain, where the master sits, dressed in blue jeans and sneakers, surrounded by Anouk Aimée, Charles Gérard, and all the other satellites.

A projectionist dashes across the room, carrying an armful of reels. In between mouthfuls, it's all shop talk—casting and locations. For once, you couldn't care less about the food. Considering it's a show-biz canteen, it's pretty good.

- o **With whom:** a starlet, of course.
- o **Where:** 15, avenue Hoche, 8th. Tel.: 42.25.00.89. You can enter freely: cross the courtyard and zip downstairs.
- o **When:** from 12:30 to 2:30 p.m.; closed Saturday and Sunday.
- o **Recommended:** tabouleh salad or tomato and mozzarella, *plat du jour* (the day's menu is announced, not written).
- o **Not recommended:** the dorado (overcooked).
- o **Welcome:** akin to Saint-Tropez.
- o **Dress:** a Davidoff cigar would be the perfect accessory.
- o **Bottom line:** see Lelouch and die happy.
- o **Cost:** 150 F.
- o **Emergency alternative:** try the cafeteria at *Salle Pleyel*, 252, rue du Faubourg St.-Honoré, 8th. (No tel.) It attracts ballet students, musicians between rehearsals, and business folk from the area.

# Le Grand Vefour

**1 p.m.**

Palais-Royal
Imperial

Many celebrities have eaten here, and not only with their lovers. Alexander Dumas and Victor Hugo dined side by side, according to a bronze commemorative plaque. Colette and Cocteau came often (but apparently sat at separate tables).

Nothing has changed at Le Grand Vefour—neither the Pompeiian friezes nor the famous paintings under glass. Revolutions, intrigues, even assassinations have failed to shake this hundred-year-old institution, which just keeps purring along, at the foot of the Palais-Royal.

And the gastronomic tradition that was launched by restaurateur Vefour, and continued by Raymond Oliver, holds up incredibly well—at incredibly high prices.

- **With whom:** a client you want to impress.
- **Where:** 17, rue du Beaujolais, 1st. Tel.: 42.96.56.27. Under the arcades of the Palais-Royal.
- **When:** from noon to 2 p.m. and 8 to 10 p.m.; closed Saturday and Sunday.
- **Recommended:** the *beignet* of lamb brains, fresh cod with curry, *croûte de noix au chocolat amer* (bittersweet chocolate cake with nut crust), Turkish coffee.
- **Welcome:** worthy of the place, right down to the cloakroom attendant and the car valet.
- **Dress:** gray flannels rather than blue jeans.
- **Bottom line:** at least once in your life. . . .
- **Cost:** fixed menu at 270 F., plus wine, for lunch only. Evening: 800 F.
- **Emergency alternative:** in the same class, *La Tour d'Argent*, 15, quai de la Tournelle, 5th. Tel.: 43.54.23.31. A special lunch menu at 250 F., plus extras. The cuisine here is truly from another era, petrified in its perfection.

# Lucas-Carton ♥

## 1 p.m.

Chef Alain Senderens has finally found a place that's as distinguished as he is, that merges the Left Bank with the Right Bank, and that integrates *nouvelle cuisine* with Art Nouveau. It's decorated with extravagant woodwork by Majorelle in sycamore and lemonwood, with bristling bouquets of wildflowers and nebulous nymphs as light fixtures (or vice versa).

The Apicius duck, poached and roasted with honey and spices, is the crowning glory of this ever-evolving cuisine, which will surely impress your clients and your most blasé acquaintances.

It must be admitted, though, that an ordinary person dropping in here might be put off by the immense dining room and irritated by the robot-like waiters in colored bow ties. For 1,000 F., one expects a little more attention.

- **With whom:** a prominent business acquaintance.
- **Where:** 9, place de la Madeleine, 8th. Tel.: 42.65.22.90. Between the boulevard Malesherbes and rue Royale.
- **When:** from noon to 3 p.m. and 8 to 10:30 p.m.; closed Saturday and Sunday.
- **Recommended:** the *menu-dégustation* (a tasting menu) and, naturally, the Apicius duck. A formidable wine list; try the Pomerol.
- **Welcome:** inattentive to common mortals.
- **Dress:** a business suit.
- **Bottom line:** a prestigious business lunch.
- **Cost:** from 700 F., if you're very careful, to over 1,000 F.
- **Emergency alternative:** *Taillevent* (p. 63).

# *Marius et Jeannette*

**1 p.m.**

The *Marius et Jeannette* trawler weighs anchor, headed for the Seychelles. Get on board, among the huge capstans, the giant hooks, and the tempting decoys that festoon the place. Hold court in the spacious wood-paneled dining room or withdraw into an adjacent stateroom.

Your mealtime "catch" will include a decor of plastic sailfish, photos of swordfish and marlin, and souvenirs of the owner's great hauls off the coast of Marseille.

There are pictures, too, of celebrities who enjoy fishing. While you dream about the briny deep, you'll be dipping into your plate and reeling in some *fines-de-claire* oysters, filets of sole, and freshly caught grilled *loup de mer* (sea bass).

- **With whom:** the old man and the sea.
- **Where:** 4, avenue George-V, 8th. Tel.: 47.23.41.88. A few steps away from the Pont de l'Alma and its riverside port.
- **When:** from noon to 2:30 p.m. and 7 to 11 p.m.; closed Saturday and Sunday.
- **Recommended:** the *fines-de-claire* oysters or the *émincé de Saint-Jacques* (thinly sliced scallops), the grilled *loup* (sea bass), the bouillabaisse.
- **Not recommended:** the *aioli* (a codfish stew), which is a little dry.
- **Welcome:** a lilting accent and a raised bottle.
- **Dress:** like an old salt, or in a business suit.
- **Bottom line:** for easy-going business appointments.
- **Cost:** 450 F.
- **Emergency alternative:** *Chez Edgard* (p. 46).

# Morot-Gaudry ♥

This Citroën garage from the 1930s—decorated with mosaics and columns, and truly a monument to the automobile—is, oddly enough, topped with a panoramic restaurant which overlooks the Eiffel Tower from a weird angle.

But is it really a restaurant? The half-hidden entrance, the intimacy of the dining room hung with peach-colored velvet, and the gracious welcome make you think you're attending a private party.

Morot-Gaudry knows exactly what it's doing: scrambled eggs with mussels, cod filet with mustard, and the dessert decorated with chevrons (a sly allusion to the Citroën symbol) are served with style and simplicity, all for 200 F. on the fixed menu—wine, coffee, and service included. A bargain!

- **With whom:** a business pal.
- **Where:** 8, rue de la Cavalerie, 15th. Tel.: 45.67.06.85. Take the elevator (barely indicated) on the left side of the entrance to the garage. Top floor.
- **When:** from noon to 2 p.m. and 7:30 to 10:30 p.m.; closed Saturday and Sunday. Reserve early to get a table on the terrace.
- **Recommended:** decide according to the day's menu; the wines are reasonable, too: I recommend the Château-Moulin-d'Arvigny 1982.
- **Welcome:** delightful.
- **Dress:** discreet and in good taste.
- **Bottom line:** a light and relaxing business lunch.
- **Cost:** 200 F. for the fixed menu, 350 F. à la carte.
- **Emergency alternative:** *Le Divellec* (p. 45).

# Le Paris

**1 p.m.**

Sèvres-Babylone
Superb

Once a pompous establishment, then a mediocre restaurant, and then a depressing tea room—the Hôtel Lutetia has finally hit its stride, thanks to a first-class facelift.

Decorator Slavik and fashion designer Sonia Rykiel have created a magnificent room that features splendid woodwork, flocked cotton fabrics, and art deco light fixtures.

Tables are well spaced, so that you can carry on serious discussions at lunch and intimate conversations at dinner. At either, your guest (male or female) will be overjoyed by the marvelous meal—and it won't cost you an arm and a leg.

- **With whom:** a publisher who needs persuading.
- **Where:** 23, rue de Sèvres, 6th. Tel.: 45.48.74.34. In the Hôtel Lutetia, which overlooks the Bon Marché department store. Free parking. Insist on the main room, not the side room.
- **When:** from noon to 2 p.m. and 7:30 to 10 p.m.; closed Sunday and Monday.
- **Recommended:** the fixed menu. For example: salmon with anis, filet of *bar* (sea perch) grilled with saffron, cheese, macaroons and coffee. Wine: Côte de Beaune.
- **Welcome:** classy.
- **Dress:** Saint Laurent Rive Gauche.
- **Bottom line:** for nonserious business.
- **Cost:** the menu at 220 F. to 350 F., complete.
- **Emergency alternative:** *Le Récamier*, across the street (p. 58).

# Le Pavillon de l'Élysée

**1 p.m.**

*Élysée*
"Savoir-boire"

Don't drink like a dunce. At the Pavillon de l'Élysée, Jean-Luc Pouteau, the best *sommelier* in the world (and therefore, French), will introduce you to his Grand Cru of the week, accompanied by a complete explanation. Did you know that the Château Capdemourlin 1979, from a chalky-clay soil, has been partially fermented in new casks, and has a complex aroma of dark fruit plus licorice, and is full-bodied . . . ?

Well, that's more than you ever wanted to know, or would dare to ask. But the Grand Cru is a pleasant pretext to indulge in a top-quality, fixed-price meal (which includes cheese but not dessert, unfortunately).

It's also a chance for you to watch the president of the Republic take his after-lunch stroll, just next door.

- **With whom:** a "nose" (that is, a wine expert).
- **Where:** 10, avenue de Champs-Élysées, 8th. Tel.: 42.65.85.10. Opposite La Grille du Coq. Parking valet at the entrance. Go upstairs; the ground floor is just the local snack place, the *Jardins de l'Élysée.*
- **When:** from noon to 2:30 p.m. and 8 to 11:30 p.m.; closed Saturday and Sunday.
- **Recommended:** a *dégustation* (tasting) menu is presented with the wine; a plate of hors-d'oeuvres, dish of the day, cheese, Lenôtre *petits fours* for dessert, and Turkish coffee.
- **Welcome:** impeccable; but why the devil do the waiters make such a big deal out of removing the dishcovers?
- **Dress:** somber attire—it's a bankers' hangout.
- **Bottom line:** to sample a variety of things.
- **Cost:** 300 F. for the menu, 600 F. à la carte (twice as expensive as the *Jardins de l'Élysée,* downstairs).
- **Emergency alternative:** *Laurent,* practically next door, at 41, avenue Gabriel, 8th. Tel.: 47.23.79.18. Same clientele; a private town house and prices to match. Bankers prefer it.

# Au Petit Riche

**1 p.m.**

Imagine the Grands Boulevards in Haussmann's day. The Opéra was under construction, the avenues were slowly getting paved, and the Petit Riche was already there, receiving gentlemen with handlebar moustaches, vests, and the red rosette of the Légion d'Honneur, who discussed stocks and bonds at lunchtime and actresses at dinner.

Now a vigorous 100 years old, the restaurant still welcomes you with the same smile, the same solemnity. If you lunch with your client in one of the comfortable private rooms, he'll feel particularly secure. And he'll become a "petit riche" himself if you handle his account with the same finesse as the restaurant handles its patrons.

- **With whom:** bankers, insurance agents, or the Drouot auction house crowd.
- **Where:** 25, rue Le Pelletier, 9th. Tel.: 47.70.68.68. At the corner of boulevard Haussmann and boulevard des Italiens, going toward rue Lafayette. Private rooms for 6 to 45 people.
- **When:** from 12:30 to 2:30 p.m. and 7:30 p.m. to 12:15 a.m.; closed Sunday.
- **Recommended:** a perfect menu at 115 F.: oysters or *rillons de Vouvray en gelée* (pork pâté in aspic), duck with turnips, a memorable warm apple pie; or, à la carte, the *boeuf gros sel* (boiled beef with coarse salt); Bourgueil and Gamay wine in carafes.
- **Welcome:** competent and helpful.
- **Dress:** a business suit.
- **Bottom line:** a comfortable and reasonable business lunch.
- **Cost:** 100 F., 150 F. if you order extras.
- **Emergency alternative:** *Le Saintongeais*, 62, rue du Faubourg-Montmartre, 9th. Tel.: 42.80.39.92. The favorite restaurant of insurance brokers.

# Le Pré Carré

**1 p.m.**

Étoile
The star system

Avenue Carnot—have you any idea where it is? It's the most nondescript little street of all those that fan out from the place de l'Étoile. And the Hôtel Splendid? It's the place where Berlusconi, the Italian TV magnate, hid out for three weeks—incognito—while he negotiated the purchase of the French network, La Cinq.

Clearly, for years now the hotel's restaurant—Le Pré Carré—has been able to protect its well-known guests from prying paparazzi.

And they're all here: the award winners, the young aspiring actors in pink cashmere sweaters, film producers and directors, television moguls, and critics. They all know each other, they wave to each other, they praise each other, they talk loudly—in Italian or American, if possible—and they manage to gulp down some adequate food. In the summer, the view of the Arc de Triomphe from the veranda makes up for the mediocrity of the sterile setting.

- **With whom:** only show-biz people.
- **Where:** 3, avenue Carnot, 17th. Tel.: 46.22.57.35. Practically under the Arc de Triomphe. Ask for a table on the veranda in the summer, or in the main dining room to make sure you're seen.
- **When:** from noon to 2:30 p.m. and 8:30 to 11 p.m.; closed Saturday and Sunday.
- **Recommended:** (more or less): *oeuf en gelée* (eggs in aspic), *faux filet* (sirloin steak; variable), the "capuccino" made with coffee ice cream.
- **Not recommended:** the *osso bucco*, the house wine.
- **Welcome:** depends on how rich and famous you are.
- **Dress:** fur or high-fashion leather.
- **Bottom line:** to find a producer.
- **Cost:** 250 F.
- **Emergency alternative:** *Sormani*, 4, rue du Général-

Lanrezac, 17th. Tel.: 43.80.13.91. Here, too, a very Parisian species is hiding out in the backroom, in the illustrious company of current celebrities. Excellent Italian cuisine, priced accordingly: 300 F. Closed Saturday and Sunday.

# Le Récamier

**1 p.m.**

Halfway between the National Assembly and the Senate, Le Récamier is the last "salon" for politicians. It's amusing, sitting in this cozy jewel-box, to count all the red rosettes of the Légion d'Honneur seated around you, to recognize this president of a nationalized company, that renowned lawyer, former minister, or a dynamic newcomer, not to mention such fixtures as Bernard-Henri Lévy (the handsome philosopher) wearing dark glasses, the better to be noticed.

A buxom hostess flirts with the still-spry senators, and a head waitress takes the orders with an air of authority; elderly waiters serve the food with extravagant respect to the notables and with quiet disdain to the un-notables.

Every region of France is represented on the menu: the *contrefilet* (sirloin roast) is cooked Bordeaux style, the calves' liver is Auvergne style, the *persillé* is Burgundy style, the potato *gratin* is Dauphinois, and the cheese selection is a kind of gastronomic gerrymandering.

The bust of Madame Récamier presides over the bar, among the bottles of scotch. It's a good bet she's enjoying herself.

o **With whom:** a political star.
o **Where:** 4, rue Récamier, 7th. Tel.: 45.48.86.58. At the end of the alleyway.
o **When:** from 12:30 to 2:30 p.m. and 8 to 10:30 p.m.; closed Sunday.
o **Recommended:** *oeufs meurette, contrefilet bordelaise, tarte fine aux pommes;* for wine, a Graves 80, *cuvée* Pierre Coste.
o **Welcome:** depends on how famous you are.
o **Dress:** wear your medals.
o **Bottom line:** to settle a case out of court, or negotiate a political platform.
o **Cost:** 350 F.

○ **Emergency alternative:** *Le Cherche-Midi*, 22, rue du Cherche-Midi, 6th. Tel.: 45.48.27.44. 150 F. Lots of good-looking people, in the friendly atmosphere of a *trattoria*.

# Le Relais Plaza

**1 p.m.**

Ladies, come display your diamonds at Le Relais Plaza; come with an elaborate Hollywood hairdo, or a fashionably disheveled coif; bring your blasé, wealthy heir, or your busy banker, or your assertive advertising account exec.

Boisterously brag about your purchases on avenue Montaigne, swoon over the most expensive melon-*tartare* in Paris, and compliment the Senegalese in a Malian costume who brings you coffee.

But don't forget to wave discreetly to Marc Bohan, Yves Saint-Laurent, and Hanae Mori at the entrance. Their presence makes the Relais the "in" place of high fashion—especially during the winter and summer collections.

- **With whom:** the leading fashion people.
- **Where:** 21, avenue Montaigne, 8th. Tel.: 47.23.46.36. In the Hôtel Plaza-Athenée. Separate entrance on the corner, across from the Comédie des Champs-Élysées. Try to get a table near the entrance; the farther back you go, the further down you'll be on the status scale.
- **When:** every day, from 11 a.m. to 1:30 a.m. A harpist at teatime; after-theater supper.
- **Recommended:** spinach salad with nuts or melon, mixed grill or *tartare*, poached pears with mint.
- **Welcome:** multilingual and efficient.
- **Dress:** overdress; wear your latest Dior creation to please Marc Bohan. Jackets required for the gentlemen.
- **Bottom line:** out of the fashion pages.
- **Cost:** 400 F. After-theater menu at 220 F.
- **Emergency alternative:** more unassuming, the *Bar des Théâtres*, just opposite (p. 67).

# La Rose des Sables

**1 p.m.**

At the entrance, there's a fountain under a starry desert sky. In the dining room, there's a Berber tent. Everywhere, there are saddles, carpets, and brass platters brought back from African campaigns. Mysterious men of the desert dressed in well-tailored blazers speak to the owner in hushed tones.

This is a luxurious bivouac. (Just imagine James Bond in the Foreign Legion.) The service is meticulous and attentive, and the chicken tagine with raisins and onions is incomparable, even by old colonial standards.

Perhaps this hushed atmosphere and the absolute discretion of the place will help you plot your next coup (on the stock market, of course).

- **With whom:** a colleague you want to baffle.
- **Where:** 19, rue Washington, 8th. Tel.: 45.63.36.73. Between the Champs-Élysées and Saint-Augustin.
- **When:** from noon to 2:30 p.m. and 7 to 11 p.m.; closed Saturday at lunch and all day Sunday.
- **Recommended:** *pastila de Fes* (pastry filled with pigeon and almonds) or *brick* (egg- or meat-filled triangular pastry), chicken tagine with raisins and onions, rather than the lamb tagine with lemon and olives; *cornes de gazelles* for dessert, mint tea.
- **Welcome:** spit 'n polish.
- **Dress:** business.
- **Bottom line:** a secret lunch.
- **Cost:** 150 F.
- **Emergency alternative:** *Flora Danica*, 142, avenue de Champs-Élysées, 8th. Tel.: 43.59.20.41. For the terrace and the "unilateral" grilled salmon (grilled on one side).

# Le Symbole

1 p.m.

République
Square

♈ ♈ ♈

There's nothing cabalistic about Le Symbole; at most, the interlaced triangle, circle, and square (its logo) are just a way of drawing attention to this smart restaurant at the République.

And people are indeed attracted to this remote neighborhood: filmmakers from nearby Gaumont, architects and fashion designers from the Marais, displaced executives. They have made Le Symbole their stomping ground, and you can understand why.

The dining room, following the latest fashion trends, wisely changed its original hi-tech décor (which was being used everywhere) and opted instead for a pared-down look, with harmonious tones of gray and graceful Italian lamps. The cuisine is refined and straightforward, and the prices are admirably restrained.

- **With whom:** a creative soul.
- **Where:** 8, rue Lucien-Sampaix, 10th. Tel.: 42.08.57.83. Place de la République, to the Bonsergent Métro. Then first street on the left.
- **When:** from noon to 3 p.m. and 8 p.m. to midnight; closed Saturday at lunch and all day Sunday.
- **Recommended:** haddock marinated in ginger. The menu changes all the time.
- **Welcome:** affected and affectionate.
- **Dress:** plenty of good buys in the neighborhood.
- **Bottom line:** add an artistic touch to your business lunch.
- **Cost:** 150 F. Excellent fixed menu at 95 F., with wine, service, and coffee included (only at lunch-time).
- **Emergency alternative:** *Jenny* (p. 171).

# *Taillevent*

**1 p.m.**

Étoile
Supreme

The name of Taillevent (Philippe de Valois' cook) has not been passed on lightly. With such a distinguished ancestry, and a worldwide clientele, this elegant town house has impeccable credentials.

The friendly owner contributes to this reputation, expertly sizing up those happy few who have been able to reserve a table and seating them like guests at court.

The cuisine, as everyone says, deserves a fourth star. The seafood *cervelas* (sausage) with truffles and pistachios, or the consommé of lobster and scallops *en gelée* (in aspic), are unpretentiously distinguished. And this extraordinary refinement is everywhere: tucked inside the celery ravioli are little chunks of lobster, as another example.

Time stands still. Some clinch business deals here; others reach nirvana.

- **With whom:** the business establishment.
- **Where:** 15, rue Lamennais, 8th. Tel.: 45.63.39.94. Near avenue Friedland. Salons on the first floor. Ask to be seated in the Louis XV salon on the ground floor.
- **When:** from 12:30 to 2 p.m. and 8 to 10:30 p.m.; closed Saturday and Sunday.
- **Recommended:** in particular, the seafood *cervelas*, the *bar* with a sweet-and-sour sauce, and the "farandole" of desserts (including, in the assortment, the famous chocolate *marquise*—a very rich chocolate cake); the best wine list in Paris.
- **Welcome:** painstaking and considerate.
- **Dress:** naturally refined.
- **Bottom line:** to get the contract signed.
- **Cost:** 600 F.
- **Emergency alternative:** *Chiberta* (p. 136).

# *Restaurant de La Trémoille* ♥

**1 p.m.**

Champs-Élysées
Disguised

Louis II, lord of La Trémoille, was apparently a perfect knight who served many kings, and who left his name on this, the most anachronistic hotel in the entire 8th arrondissement.

For who would want to venture into this barren provincial-style dining room just to nibble on an over-cooked green-bean salad and a piteously prepared filet of sole?

True, the fireplace is homey and hospitable, and the service—though clumsy—has good intentions. (The waiters remind you of château caretakers who are merely dressed up as maîtres d'). The wine list badly needs updating. However, you *can* converse in peace here: that's the advantage of lunching in an unknown restaurant where the tables are far apart.

- **With whom:** ssh!
- **Where:** 12, rue de La Trémoille, 8th. Tel.: 47.23.34.20. Between avenue George-V and rue François-Ier.
- **When:** every day, like any hotel restaurant.
- **Recommended:** curb your sense of adventure; take, for example, a mixed salad, a *croque-monsieur* or a Bresse chicken, and a chocolate mousse. One nice surprise on the wine list: a Haut-Marbuzet 1975 at 170 F.
- **Welcome:** a little clumsy but well-meaning.
- **Dress:** like a guest of the hotel.
- **Bottom line:** for various kinds of bargaining.
- **Cost:** 250 F.
- **Emergency alternative:** discretion also assured at the Hôtel Lancaster, 7, rue de Berri, 8th. Tel.: 43.59.90.43. In the summer there's a delightful terrace. Fixed menu at 190 F.

# Feeding the Body Politic

Any French politician worth his salt knows that the way to your opponent's heart is through his stomach. Fittingly, the restaurants around the National Assembly practice "cohabitation"—just like the French government itself.

*Chez Françoise:* aérogare des Invalides, 7th. Tel.: 47.05.49.03. Nobody can accuse the Socialist deputies of having expensive taste: the fixed menu here costs only 115 F., served in awful surroundings below street level. The ambience is secretive and silent as a committee meeting room; the main items on the agenda are filet of beef with red butter, and roast pigeon. Closed Sunday evening and Monday. ♈

*Chez Marius:* 5, rue de Bourgogne, 7th. Tel.: 47.05.96.19. Thoroughly ecumenical, this is the refuge of the "refuzniks"—those who avoid eating at the National Assembly canteen. It's a stone's throw from the Assembly and the headquarters of the Socialist Party . . . but as for having a good lunch. . . . ♈

*Les Glénan:* 54, rue de Bourgogne, 7th. Tel.: 45.51.61.09. Run by Michel Giraud, a short hop away from the Regional Council, this place is neutral ground for final arbitration between government ministers and councillors. Figure 250 F., or a top-quality gastronomic menu at 140 F. Closed Saturday at midday and all day Sunday. ♈ ♈

*La Gauloise:* 59, avenue de la Motte-Picquet, 15th. Tel.: 47.34.11.64. Very Radical Socialist and Freemason, this place was a favorite of the top people in the Socialist government—at least until the elections of March 1986, which brought back the Conservative-Right. But this oldtime brasserie goes on, and its *salade*

*landaise* has plenty of political clout. 280 F. Closed
Saturday and Sunday.

*La Marlotte:* 55, rue du Cherche-Midi, 6th. Tel.:
45.48.86.79. A very cozy cottage that doesn't conceal
its predilection for the new Conservative-Right majori-
ty. Valéry Giscard d'Estaing celebrates his birthdays
there, and Jacques Chirac, in an autographed photo,
extends his "cordial regards." The menu is changed
constantly, but the *carré* of lamb and the Charolais beef
are perennial pleasures. 150 F.

# Le Bar des Théâtres ♥

## 1 p.m.

Le Bar des Théâtres doesn't live off only the theater crowd and their late-night suppers. Mainly it's a rendezvous for worldly spectators, for models from avenue Montaigne, stars from Antenne 2 television, and perhaps heiresses from the Plaza-Athénée.

At noon you'll think you're at an art opening because it's so hard to beat your way to a free table, and because everyone is so ridiculously overdressed.

The dignified waiter who calls all his customers "Monsieur le Président" (he's not always mistaken) is very proud of his cold salmon with mayonnaise. Stick to simple things: order melon (in season), a *tartare*, and a voluptuous mound of *chantilly* (whipped cream) on fresh raspberries or on anything else.

- **With whom:** a top model or a television star.
- **Where:** 6, avenue Montaigne, 8th. Tel.: 47.23.34.63. Opposite the Théâtre des Champs-Élysées.
- **When:** from 6 a.m. to 2 a.m. every day.
- **Recommended:** chilled melon or salad niçoise, *tartare* or calves' liver, raspberries Melba.
- **Not recommended:** cold salmon with mayonnaise, chocolate cake.
- **Welcome:** simple but rushed.
- **Dress:** something you've recently bought on avenue Montaigne.
- **Bottom line:** a fashion-magazine lunch.
- **Cost:** 150 F.
- **Emergency alternative:** *Chez Pepita*, 21, rue Bayard, 8th. Tel.: 47.23.58.49. From 9 a.m. to 9:30 p.m., except Saturday and Sunday. Opposite R.T.L. radio, it attracts more truck drivers than celebrities. Typically Parisian chatter, and super-fast service.

# Le Blue Fox Bar ♥

Once a modest furshop, Le Blue Fox always had a taste for luxury. It was turned into a popular wine bar by an enterprising Englishman, who is naturally inclined toward the châteaux of Claret—pictures of which decorate the upstairs room, alongside instructive posters about bread, wine, and coffee.

International bankers and lawyers don't hesitate to drop their clients and run off to meet their lovers here; it's conveniently located between Hermès and Burberry's. While waiting, they read the only newspaper available, *The Financial Times.*

Athletic and weight-conscious, they settle for a salad with haddock filets (nearly raw and very tender). But often their resistance weakens at the sight of the fruit crumble (fruit with a crumb-topping)—by far the best dessert in the house.

- **With whom:** a beautiful woman, laden with shopping bags.
- **Where:** 25, rue Royale, 8th. Tel.: 42.65.10.72. Between 25, rue Royale and 24, rue Boissy-d'Anglas, near the Madeleine.
- **When:** from 10 a.m. to 10 p.m.; closed Saturday evening and Sunday.
- **Recommended:** salad with haddock filets or paprika chicken, fruit crumble.
- **Not recommended:** Mexican salad, quiche.
- **Welcome:** well-mannered.
- **Dress:** like the locals.
- **Bottom line:** for a gallant, but galloping, rendezvous.
- **Cost:** 120 F.
- **Emergency alternative:** in a pinch, the cafeteria at *Fauchon*, 28, place Madeleine, 8th. Tel.: 47.42.60.11.

# Dragons-Élysée

*1 p.m.*

Shanghai in the 1930s. Plaster dragons and plastic Buddhas, metal stairs and shiny ceilings, glass shelves and mirrored walls. Clearly, no expense has been spared to indulge every cliché of the Asian *nouveaux-riches.*

You walk past fish tanks and a splashing waterfall, and then choose from the specialties of two chefs—one Thai, the other Chinese.

It's all served with great care and reverence, and costs only 70 F., including warm washcloths and the tip.

- **With whom:** business buddies.
- **Where:** 11, rue de Berri, 8th. Tel.: 42.89.85.10. A hop away from the Champs-Élysées, next to the City Rock Café.
- **When:** every day until 11:30 p.m.
- **Recommended:** only at noon—spicy Thai soup, chicken with almonds, Cantonese rice, apple fritters.
- **Welcome:** attentive.
- **Dress:** As you like; they're tolerant here.
- **Bottom line:** An exotic journey for the price of a Chinese meal.
- **Cost:** 150 F. At noon, fixed menus at 70 F. and 198 F.
- **Emergency alternative:** *Au Mandarin,* 1, rue de Berri, 8th. Tel.: 43.59.48.48. Fixed menu at 60 F. and 96 F. An equally flashy décor, including a plastic empress on a cloud. *La Cascade Chinoise,* 7, rue de Ponthieu, 8th. Tel.: 45.61.93.63. An indoor fountain, a hushed silence, and top-notch cuisine for 150 F.

# L'Écluse

**1 p.m.**

Formerly, L'Écluse was a place that promoted new, talented singers; now it promotes the time-honored virtues of Bordelais and regional specialties.

Though reincarnated several times, the décor has remained faithful to the style of an oldtime bistro (oak bar, 1900-style posters, red banquettes, mirrored walls), and the restaurant's light fare has gradually caught on among late-night gourmets looking for a mini-supper.

But L'Écluse is equally good for a quick lunch, as long as you don't mind noise and confusion, especially if you despair of ever finding a restaurant on the drab Champs-Élysées.

Follow up the *foie gras maison* (accompanied by a glass of sauterne) with a carpaccio (accompanied by a Médoc) some chèvre cheese (with a Saint-Émilion), and last of all, the famous chocolate cake (with a glass of water: wine-tasting has its limits).

- **With whom:** a co-worker will do.
- **Where:** 64, rue François-Ier, 8th. Tel.: 47.20.77.09. Between the defunct Nova Park Hotel and avenue George-V. Also, three others in the chain: 15, quai des Grands-Augustins, 6th. Tel.: 46.33.58.74 (the original one). 15, place de la Madeleine, 8th. Tel.: 42.65.34.09. 2, rue du Général Henrion Bertier, 92200 Neuilly. Tel.: 46.24.21.06.
- **When:** every day from noon to 2 a.m.
- **Recommended:** *foie gras*, goose filets, chocolate cake; an informative but illegible wine list.
- **Not recommended:** the *tartare.*
- **Welcome:** à la bistro.
- **Dress:** your work duds.
- **Bottom line:** for some *foie gras*, chocolate cake, and bordeaux at any hour.
- **Cost:** 150 F.

- **Emergency alternative:** the restaurant at the *Théâtre du Rond-Point*, avenue Franklin Roosevelt, 8th. Tel.: 42.56.22.01. It's not good, but it's not expensive, and you'll run into Jean-Louis Barrault and other theater types.

# L'Entrecôte

**1 p.m.**

Why in the world is L'Entrecôte also called "Relais de Venise" (the Venetian Inn)? A few gondolas naïvely painted on the wall are hardly enough to create that illusion.

This place is quintessentially French, catering to medium-rare, middle-class Frenchmen who eagerly jam in out of habit, out of thriftiness, and out of appreciation for quality.

They're not disappointed. The Entrecôte formula is internationally known and copied, but it's here, at the parent establishment, that you'll find the best french fries and the one-and-only authentic steak sauce. The *vacherin au chocolat* (ice-cream-topped meringue) and the other desserts are as impressive as they are delectable. Service is always fast and attentive.

Come at noon if you want to avoid a long wait on line.

- **With whom:** an old friend.
- **Where:** 271, boulevard Pereire, 17th. (No tel.) Past the train station on the line that circles the city, at the corner of rue du Débarcadère.
- **When:** from noon to 2 p.m. and 7 to 10 p.m. Less of a wait at lunchtime; no reservations.
- **Recommended:** the standard formula: salad, *entrecôte*, and *frites;* then perhaps a *vacherin.*
- **Welcome:** hospitable, competent, fast.
- **Dress:** things you've bought on sale.
- **Bottom line:** a hefty lunch that's quickly served.
- **Cost:** 100 F.
- **Emergency alternative:** *Le Petit Salé*, 99, avenue des Ternes, 17th. Tel.: 45.74.10.57.

# L'Espace ♥

Concorde
Stars

Pierre Cardin entertains with style. His Espace, decorated with neon floral motifs, is above all designed to please his friends from the world of fashion and the theater. Big posters and portraits of stars surround the temptingly fresh and copious buffet spread.

Leading names in the French entertainment field regularly turn up here, including popular television newscasters.

In the summer, these birds of paradise chirp happily in their gilded cage in the garden, and peer through the chestnut trees to watch the tourists on the Champs-Élysées.

- **With whom:** a fragile model from Cardin.
- **Where:** 1, avenue Gabriel, 8th. Tel.: 42.66.11.70. Between the Élysée Palace and the place de la Concorde, down the street from the American Embassy.
- **When:** every day, except Saturday at noon, from 12:15 to 3 p.m. and 8:30 p.m. to 2 a.m. In the summer, a delightful garden.
- **Recommended:** the nonstop buffet (*crudités*, tabouleh, herring, various desserts); the *plat du jour* is not recommended.
- **Welcome:** overly effusive.
- **Dress:** high fashion, of course.
- **Bottom line:** a worldly buffet.
- **Cost:** 120 F.; 170 F. if you also take the *plat du jour*.
- **Emergency alternative:** the restaurant at the *Théâtre du Rond-Point*, avenue Franklin Roosevelt, 8th. Tel.: 42.56.22.01.

# Rose Thé ♥

## 1 p.m.

♈ ♈ ♈

Rose Thé is feminine but not effete. You can make an appointment there with any virile advertising executive, or any eccentric artist, without the slightest sense of embarrassment. You won't find any "girls" here, but rather, professional women like the one who runs the place: mature, attractive, and a little pushy.

Nestled at the rear of a turn-of-the-century antiques gallery, this pretty nook stresses comfort. The regular customers gratefully sink into their leather armchairs, nearly slipping under the table.

They rediscover the pleasures of a light meal, settling for a savory tart and *fromage blanc* with almonds and honey. A cup of tea is the final dietetic touch.

- **With whom:** a businesswoman.
- **Where:** 91, rue Saint-Honoré, 1st. Tel.: 42.36.97.18. At the rear of the antiques gallery.
- **When:** from noon to 6:30 p.m.; closed Saturday and Sunday. Reserve for lunch.
- **Recommended:** tart and salad of the day, *fromage blanc* with almonds and honey, cheesecake.
- **Welcome:** charming and personal.
- **Dress:** something a little retro.
- **Bottom line:** a calm, chatty lunch.
- **Cost:** 70 F.
- **Emergency alternative:** *Le Potiron*, 16, rue du Roule, 1st. Tel.: 42.33.35.68. First-rate cooking.

# *Willi's*

Palais-R

Willi's may be the number-one wine bar in Paris, and certainly it's the most British. It's the only one that actually measures up to its gastronomic goals, and that is a hit with both avant-garde fashion designer Jean-Paul Gaultier and top Chanel model Ines de La Fressange.

The manager, a distinguished and discriminating oenologue, helps his clients and friends choose their wine and insists on serving it himself, explaining the correct way to taste it. His efficient and "proper" waiters (they must have gone to Eton or Harrow) serve excellent dishes that are as good as the wine they accompany.

The décor is unpretentious: a bar, exposed beams, empty wine bottles displayed on the shelves, attractive paintings, and—of all things—a poster that advertises Napa Valley sauvignon. Dry British humor.

o **With whom:** a banker who can relax long enough for a meal.

o **Where:** 13, rue des Petits-Champs, 1st. Tel.: 42.61.05.09. Opposite the Bibliothèque Nationale.

o **When:** from 11 a.m. to 11 p.m. Closed Sunday. Livelier at noon.

o **Recommended:** mozzarella with crushed tomatoes, roasted chevreau (kid) with rosemary or beef with green beans, cheese platter, chocolate terrine. And, of course, a Côtes-du-Rhône.

o **Welcome:** cordial and reserved; the best British manners.

o **Dress:** your old college tie.

o **Bottom line:** a quick, friendly lunch with good wine.

o **Cost:** 150 F.

o **Emergency alternative:** *Chez Georges*, 1, rue du Mail, 2nd. Tel.: 42.60.07.11. Celery *rémoulade*, calves' liver, and marvelous *tarte Tatin* for the

.ashion designers of the place des Victoires, the journalists of *Le Figaro* and *Le Nouvel Observateur*, and the stockbrokers from the Bourse. Up to you to tell them apart. Figure about 200 F. *Le Louis XIV*, 1 bis, place des Victoires, 1st. Tel.: 42.61.39.44. The same crowd, a notch more expensive, and not any better.

# Afternoon

*Coffee Break*
*Tea*
*Cocktails*

# Chez Basile

*Saint-Germain*
French Ivy League

The waiters are devoted to both their job and the students who come here. As if by osmosis, they've picked up bits of college courses and undergraduate habits, and they treat the lecturers and professors with all due deference. (The school in question is Sciences Politiques, familiarly known as Sciences Po—one of France's *"grandes écoles."*)

The pinball machine here isn't very popular; the main attraction is the bar, which serves heavy doses of espresso to those who are marginally matriculated and to those who are conscientiously cramming.

The regulars at Chez Basile—senior students, sexy young things, and militant social workers—drown themselves in gallons of coffee in the front room, use the familiar *"tu"* to their favorite waiter (who doesn't reciprocate), and talk at the top of their lungs—perhaps to your amusement.

- **With whom:** a student from Sciences Po or a friend who wants to meet one.

- **Where:** 34, rue de Grenelle, 7th. Tel.: 42.22.59.46. Opposite Sciences Po, at the corner of rue Grenelle and rue Saint-Guillaume.

- **When:** from 7 a.m. to 8:30 p.m.; closed Sunday.

- **Recommended:** *café crème*, and possibly the *plat du jour.*

- **Not recommended:** the commercially made pastries.

- **Welcome:** grandiose.

- **Dress:** a well-knotted tie.

- **Bottom line:** the rendez-vous of Sciences-Im-Posters.

- **Cost:** 5 F.

○ **Emergency alternative:** for a cup of coffee with an operatic background, *Christian Constant*, 26, rue du Bac, 7th. Tel.: 42.96.53.53; or the *Café de la Mairie*, 8, place Saint-Sulpice, 6th. Tel.: 43.26.67.82. For suntanning on the terrace.

# *Brocco*

Back in 1880, Monsieur Brocco must have been a megalomaniac. Either wanting to honor the recently created Republic, or simply wanting to show off his new prosperity, he built himself the most monumental pastry shop in Paris: decorated with marble, onyx, *faux* Corinthian columns, and topped off by an ethereal goddess on the ceiling.

One hundred years later, a contented owner is still reigning behind the counter, proud of his establishment, while his neighborhood customers automatically order a *café crème* and luscious fresh-baked pastries. Among them are some bedazzled tourists, assiduously tracking down the "real" Paris.

- **With whom:** a tourist you want to impress.
- **Where:** 180, rue du Temple, 3rd. Tel.: 42.72.19.81. A short hop away from place de la République.
- **When:** every day from 7 a.m. to 7:45 p.m.
- **Recommended:** croissants, *pains au chocolat*, meringues, *café crème*.
- **Not recommended:** the more complicated pastries, the teabag tea.
- **Welcome:** efficient, but distant.
- **Dress:** unpretentious.
- **Bottom line:** a monumental café.
- **Cost:** 6 F. for a *café crème*, less than 10 F. for a pastry.
- **Emergency alternative:** *Au Petit Fer à Cheval* (p. 82).

# La Buvette du Musée Rodin ♥

## 3 p.m.

In France, to raise your child properly, you start early and you start here—shielding him from joggers, roller skaters, and other sportsmen, and encouraging him instead to distinguish Rodin's *Thinker* from his statue of Balzac.

This, the most exclusive garden in Paris (you have to pay 2 F. to get in), affords protection against all and sundry, while the maid, the nanny, or the *au pair* sips a cup of coffee (but knows better than to have one of the awful pastries).

- **With whom:** a young mother and her baby carriage.
- **Where:** 77, rue de Varenne, 7th. Tel.: 47.05.01.34. Between rue de Bourgogne and the Invalides.
- **When:** from 10 a.m. to 5:45 p.m. Closed Tuesday.
- **Recommended:** a Coke or coffee, if you really need it.
- **Not recommended:** everything else.
- **Welcome:** curt.
- **Dress:** upscale suburban.
- **Bottom line:** better than going to a day nursery.
- **Cost:** 3 F. for coffee.
- **Emergency alternative:** *Pradier*, 32, rue de Bourgogne, 7th. Tel.: 45.51.72.37. A pastry shop that vaguely resembles a tea room. Excellent macaroons and apple nougat.

# Au Petit Fer à Cheval

## 3 p.m.

This turn-of-the-century café cultivates a folkloric kind of chic, with a lavish bar made of horseshoes, wood banquettes from the Métro, and old percolators.

Regular customers mix with the neighborhood's new gentrified residents and with the gays who frequent this street at night.

If you're disappointed in your *café crème*, try perking it up with a remarkable *amandine poire cassis* pastry that comes from Tout au Beurre across the street—a tiny pastry shop that deserves to be included in your itinerary.

- **With whom:** someone who wants to see some local color.
- **Where:** 30, rue Vieille-du-Temple, 4th. Tel.: 42.72.47.47. On the rue de Rivoli side.
- **When:** from 7:30 a.m. to 2 a.m.; closed Sunday.
- **Recommended:** the *café crème* (very ordinary). Perhaps, in the backroom, some crudités and a *boudin* (sausage).
- **Welcome:** pleasant.
- **Dress:** come as you are.
- **Bottom line:** a superb café, larger-than-life Parisian.
- **Cost:** 3.50 F. for coffee at the counter.
- **Emergency alternative:** *Le Temps des Cerises* (p. 83).

# Le Temps des Cerises

## 3 p.m.

*Marais*
Retro

Stop for a moment in front of this fragile building, with its slate roof, its zinc raingutters, and its big dormer windows: it could be home to an oldtime millionaire.

Behind this gray façade you might well expect to enter a lush Vuillard interior. But the fact is, this former administration building, owned by the Celestine Convent and transformed into a tavern, remains as pure and simple as it appears in a photograph taken in 1914.

The family-style dinner, limited in choice and served in haste, costs only 42 F. But instead of that, why not take a breather at the bar with a glass of the house wine or a good simple coffee.

- **With whom:** the guys.
- **Where:** 31, rue de la Cerisaie, 4th. Tel.: 42.72.08.63. Very close to the Hôtel de Sens.
- **When:** the bar: from 7:30 a.m. to 8 p.m.; the restaurant: from 11:30 a.m. to 2:30 p.m.; closed Saturday and Sunday.
- **Recommended:** either the menu at 42 F. with a pitcher of the house wine at 27 F., or—better—just a simple coffee.
- **Welcome:** youthful and friendly.
- **Dress:** a beret.
- **Bottom line:** a timeless cup of coffee.
- **Cost:** 5 F. for the coffee.
- **Emergency alternative:** *Au Petit Fer à Cheval* (p. 82).

# *Verlet*

Dating back to 1880, this little brandy distillery on rue Saint-Honoré would have appealed to Emile Zola, both for its bustling atmosphere and the sure hand of Monsieur Verlet, whose great-grandfather sold exotic spices that had been brought back from India by clipper ship. Even today the mere sight of the old tea caddies on the shelves and the large sacks of coffee in the window are proof enough that this is Paris's leading specialist in teas and coffees. If you let him, Verlet will give your coffee break a gastronomic dimension. Trust his expert advice, or sniff out some beans from Kenya or Colombia on your own. Accompany it with a melting chocolate charlotte and you'll swear never again to drink an ordinary cup of restaurant coffee after lunch.

- **With whom:** your lunch companion.
- **Where:** 256, rue Saint-Honoré, 1st. Tel.: 42.60.67.39. Near the Théâtre Français.
- **When:** from 9 a.m. to 7 p.m.; closed Saturday and Sunday.
- **Recommended:** all the coffees are good, especially the one from Kenya.
- **Welcome:** competent and helpful.
- **Dress:** business.
- **Bottom line:** a perfect ending to lunch in the neighborhood.
- **Cost:** 5.50 F. for coffee.
- **Emergency alternative:** none; better just to wait here for a seat.

# Meeting Places:
# Outdoors/Indoors

## Champs-Élysées

Artcurial: 9, avenue Matignon, 8th. Tel.: 42.56.70.70.
An art gallery and bookstore.

Le marché aux timbres (outdoor stamp market):
Thursday, Saturday, and Sunday at the corner of avenue
Matignon and avenue Gabriel, 8th.

La Clepsydre, in the Claridge Gallery: 74, avenue des
Champs-Élysées, 8th.

The permanent collections in the Petit Palais (Musée
des Beaux-Arts de la Ville de Paris): avenue Alexandre
III, 8th.

The courtyard waterfall at Prunier: 26, avenue des
Champs-Élysées, 8th.

Hôtel de la Païva: avenue des Champs-Élysées, 8th.
Visits permitted between 10 and 11 a.m. on Sunday.

## Beaubourg–Les Halles

The Brancusi studio: attached to the Centre Pompidou,
4th.

The Tinguely/Niki de Saint-Phalle pond: wedged
between the Centre Pompidou and the Saint-Merri
church, 4th.

Moretti's fresco: third floor of the Forum des Halles,
rue des Pilliers, 1st.

The Saint-Eustache church: 1st.

The Saint-Jacques tower: 1st.

The Arts et Metiers library: in the nave of the chapel,
3rd.

## Marais

The Marché-Sainte-Catherine square: between rue de
Sévigné and rue Turenne, 3rd.

Victor Hugo's house: 6, place des Vosges, 3rd.

The Parc-Royal square: rue du Parc-Royal, 3rd.

The inner courtyard of the Hôtel de Sully: 62, rue
Saint-Antoine, 3rd.

The Vieux Paris bookstore: 62, rue François-Miron,
4th.

The Arsenal Library: 1, rue Sully, 4th. Full of histori-
cal documents.

## Saint-Germain–Quartier Latin

The Pont des Arts: the bridge between the Louvre and
the Academy, 1st.

The Mazarine Library: quai de Conti, 1st. (Easy to get
a card here.)

The Shakespeare and Co. bookstore: quai de Monte-
bello and rue Saint-Jacques, 5th.

La Hune gallery and bookstore: next to Aux Deux
Magots, 6th.

The place Furstenberg: in front of the Delacroix
Museum (or in the museum garden), 6th.

The cour de Rohan: just off rue Saint-André-des-Arts,
6th.

## The Islands: La Cité and Saint-Louis

The Vert Galant square: 1st.

The l'Île-de-France square: behind Notre-Dame, 1st.
The Salle des Pas Perdus: at the Palais de Justice, 1st.
The Polish Library: 6, quai d'Orléans, 1st.
Behind one of the pillars of the Saint-Louis church,
1st.

## Opéra–Palais Royal

The pond at the Palais Royal: 1st.

The statue of *The Three Graces*, by Maillol: in the
Louvre garden, 1st.

The place des Victoires: at Kenzo, for example, 1st.
Hachette-Opéra: place de l'Opéra, 2nd. In front of the
huge video screen.

The Cité Bergère: at any of its hotels (behind Le
Palace), 9th.

## Montmartre

The P.M.U. hotel: impasse de la Défense, 22 avenue de
Clichy, 9th.

The garden of the Thiers Library: 9th.
The Gustave-Moreau Museum: 9th.
The Montmartre vineyard: 18th.
The Bateau-Lavoir: place Émile-Goudeau, at the end
of rue Ravignan, 18th.

The rue Lepic: 18th (on a market day).
The Château des Brouillards: 13, rue Girardon, 18th.

Souvenirs of the deranged French writer Gérard de Nerval.

## Montparnasse-Invalides

Zadkine Museum: 100 bis, rue d'Assas, 7th. Bucolic and all-but-forgotten.
  "Casino": corner of rue de la Gaîté, 14th. Open air.
  The Art Nouveau building: 29, avenue Rapp, 7th.
  Entrance to the Montparnasse Squash Club: on the Montparnasse esplanade, 14th.

## 16th Arrondissement

The Palais de Tokyo: on the steps.
  The Bagatelle Garden.
  The Balzac Museum: 47, rue Raynouard.
  The Museum of French Monuments: in front of the statue of *La Marseillaise* by Rude. A dusty and romantic place.
  The Lycée Janson: at the end of the school day.
  The Théâtre de Ranelagh: for oldtimers hamming it up.

## Avoid at all costs:

Meeting on the steps of the Opera House, at the statue of Danton at place de l'Odéon, on the Beaubourg "plateau," in the entrance hall of F.N.A.C. (the big discount store), in the middle of the place de la Concorde, in front of the heavily guarded Élysée Palace or Israeli Embassy, the Quai des Orfèvres (the central police station); at night under the Pont-Neuf, or at Porte-Dauphine and Porte-Saint-Denis (prostitutes' pickup places).

# Carette ♥

Preppies, Sloane Rangers, or Parisian "minets"? There are many ways to classify the high school kids who come here—kids who attend, and flunk out of, the best schools in the city.

They're a privileged bunch. They've given up the petitions and protests of the last generation in favor of nightclubbing. They seem less inspired by the verses of Paul Valéry (carved on the façade of the Musée de l'Homme, just opposite Carette) than by the subtle distinctions among favored discothèques.

Teeny-boppers and their motorcycling boyfriends meet here on the terrace, inside in the ornately decorated room, or between the two, under the awning. They spend an hour or so together, chatting and eyeing the convertible that has just pulled up. In most respects, they're like their American counterparts: children of a consumer society.

- **With whom:** a minor . . . from a good background.
- **Where:** 4, place du Trocadéro, 16th. Tel.: 47.27.88.56. The busy terrace, near avenue Kléber.
- **When:** from 8 a.m. to 7 p.m.; closed Tuesday.
- **Recommended:** the Mont-Blanc sundae is tops, but so is the macaroon with chocolate, the tarte Tatin, and the coffee parfait.
- **Welcome:** affluent.
- **Dress:** a Benetton sweater over a pink Lacoste shirt.
- **Bottom line:** indulge in a Mont-Blanc sundae among French preppies.
- **Cost:** 40 F.
- **Emergency alternative:** *Coquelin Aîné*, 67, rue de Passy, 16th. Tel.: 42.88.21.74.

# La Cour de Rohan ♥

**5 p.m.**

Soft chamber music fills every corner of La Cour de Rohan. After you get used to the style and elegance of the ground floor, which looks out onto a French garden, go up the glass-enclosed staircase to the more intimate —and more British—first floor.

Smartly dressed students and music-lovers have adopted this place as their own: it's certainly more fun and more agreeable to meet here than under Danton's statue, on a littered street nearby.

You'll feel as though you're visiting an elderly aunt from Brighton, who is using her best china and serving you her best brioche, from the sideboard once owned by Jean Cocteau. The owner is actually a much younger woman, but just as charming.

- **With whom:** a shy lover you want to put at ease.
- **Where:** 59–61, rue Saint-André-des-Arts, 6th. Tel.: 43.25.79.67. From place de l'Odéon, take the arcade toward rue Saint-André-des-Arts. Go upstairs.
- **When:** from noon to 7 p.m., on Saturday and Sunday from 2 p.m.; closed Monday. Busy over the weekend.
- **Recommended:** the cake with three kinds of chocolate, charlottes, brioche, hot chocolate, or China tea.
- **Welcome:** ravishing.
- **Dress:** discreet and in good taste.
- **Bottom line:** music, charm, calm.
- **Cost:** 60 F.
- **Emergency alternative:** *Fanny Tea* (p. 90).

# *Fanny Tea* ♥

## 5 p.m.

Let's be honest—Fanny doesn't always make things easy. She tends to butt in on conversations, and will even upbraid a customer who dares to smoke or talk too loudly.

But her tea room is delightfully arranged: volumes of poetry on the tables let you pass the time while waiting for a friend to arrive, and the teas and pies are always of the highest quality.

Fanny operates this place like a little literary salon: her strong personality, the bookish ambience, and the intimacy of the old-fashioned setting are perfect.

- **With whom:** a gentle art student.
- **Where:** 20, place Dauphine, 1st. Tel.: 43.25.83.67. On the square, facing the Left Bank (Rive Gauche).
- **When:** from 1 to 7:30 p.m., on Sunday from 3:30 to 8 p.m.; closed Monday.
- **Recommended:** tea (made with well water), apple pie, pear pie, lemon mousse.
- **Welcome:** remember, you're a guest.
- **Dress:** like Bernard Pivot, on his literary TV show (i.e., tweedy).
- **Bottom line:** for conversation, sharing secrets.
- **Cost:** 60 F.
- **Emergency alternative:** *La Cour de Rohan* (p. 89).

# Je Thé . . . me

## 5 p.m.

Je Thé . . . me (a play on the words *je t'aime*) is a place for people who love tea and who love each other. This neighborhood shop, whose walls are lined with wood shelves reaching up to the ceiling, was once a deluxe but austere grocery store.

Thanks to the cute Japanese dolls tucked away here and there, and the charming smile of the young owner, the whole atmosphere has changed.

The traditional specialties are excellent, which is why there's always a big crowd happy to jam into this unpretentious place.

- **With whom:** a relaxed intellectual, if you know one.
- **Where:** 4, rue d'Alleray, 15th. Tel.: 48.42.48.30. At the corner of rue Vaugirard.
- **When:** from noon to 7 p.m.; closed Sunday.
- **Recommended:** *fondant au chocolat* (a fudge cake), amandines (little cakes made with almonds), and various tarts.
- **Welcome:** cordial, even friendly.
- **Dress:** a turtleneck.
- **Bottom line:** provincial gentility.
- **Cost:** 40 F.
- **Emergency alternative:** *La Cour de Rohan* (p. 89).

# Société Théosophique de France

*Champ de Mars*
Metaphysical

*5 p.m.*

A rendez-vous at the Theosophical Society of France is essential for anyone who dreams of universal amity and who is seeking to penetrate the mysteries of human destiny. You'll find yourself in the majestic hall—half thermal baths, half mosque—decorated in a great cosmic burst of interlaced religious and mystical symbols.

Or you can pass the time in the library discovering the secrets of vegetarianism, yoga, Zen, Krishnamurti, gnosticism, and other esoteric disciplines.

Better yet, go for five o'clock tea. But you'll have to pay the price: piously participating in a class on "Theosophy and the Age of Aquarius" or "The Earth Mother in Different Religions."

- **With whom:** an introspective friend.
- **Where:** 4, square Rapp, 7th. At the corner of 35, avenue Rapp, near rue Saint-Dominique. Tel.: 45.51.31.79.
- **When:** Saturday for tea at 5 p.m. after the class, and Sunday at 5 p.m. after the lecture.
- **Recommended:** a "concentrated" tea.
- **Welcome:** absorbed and inspired.
- **Dress:** ethereal.
- **Bottom line:** who are we, where do we come from, where are we going?
- **Cost:** 5 F. for the class, 20 F. for the lecture.
- **Emergency alternative:** *Le Petit Boule*, 12, avenue de la Motte-Picquet, 7th. Tel.: 45.51.77.48.

# *Thé Dansant at La Coupole*  ♥

## 5 p.m.

A big band—like oldtime Lester Lanin—plays nonstop in this dark, subterranean dance hall. The maître d', wearing a wide bow tie, will only allow entrance to gentlemen in jackets and ties and to properly attired ladies.

At the first notes of the accordion, couples throw themselves into a tango or a paso doble, just as they did in their youth. The ladies sway in their partners' arms, never letting themselves go completely.

Ladies, be careful! If you're meeting someone here, don't arrive too early. Some of these men, especially the younger ones, might get ideas.

- **With whom:** your mother's best friend.
- **Where:** 102, boulevard Montparnasse, 14th. Tel.: 43.20.14.20. Under La Coupole restaurant.
- **When:** every day from 4:30 p.m. to 2 a.m.
- **Recommended:** a cup of tea will suffice.
- **Welcome:** high-camp pomposity.
- **Dress:** any old tie, but definitely a tie.
- **Bottom line:** organized infidelity.
- **Cost:** 60 F.
- **Emergency alternative:** tea dances at *L'Étoile*, 2 bis, avenue Foch, 16th. Tel.: 45.00.00.13.

# *Toraya*

Concorde
Ceremonial

Parisians have no idea how lucky they are to have, right in their city, the only foreign showcase of Japan's most prestigious pastry establishment, purveyors to His Majesty the Emperor for 450 years.

The four spiritual principles of the tea ceremony—harmony, respect, purity, and tranquility—demand a sober décor: smoked glass, black lacquered tables, an abstract "minimalist" tapestry.

Following the rules of tradition, your Japanese lover will order a Matcha—a strong, mossy emulsion of tea—sweetened by a very dry, sugary cake. More cautious, you'll prefer a thirst-quenching ceremonial green tea, accompanied by a Yokan (a traditional sweet bean cake), delicately served with a hand-carved wooden pick.

- **With whom:** a Japanese lover, or a distinguished woman.
- **Where:** 10, rue Saint-Florentin, 1st. Tel.: 42.60.13.00. Near place de la Concorde, between rue Saint-Honoré and rue de Rivoli.
- **When:** from 10 a.m. to 7 p.m.; closed Sunday.
- **Recommended:** the list is in Japanese; choose the Yokan and the green tea (more thirst-quenching than the Matcha).
- **Welcome:** meticulous and ceremonious.
- **Dress:** Madame Butterfly.
- **Bottom line:** a most refined tea.
- **Cost:** 25 F.
- **Emergency alternative:** *Ladurée* (p. 97).

# Smith, Angelina,
# Le Meurice ♥

## 5 p.m.

Tea-time is synonymous with the rue de Rivoli: a stroll with grandma in the Tuileries leads you naturally to Smith, a visit to the Louvre takes you to Angelina, and shopping excursions under the Rivoli arcade end up at the Meurice.

You can choose a tea-time that will be British and chatty, Belle Epoque and worldly, or stately, accompanied by the strains of a piano—but it will always be dignified, traditional, and cosmopolitan.

*W. H. Smith & Son:* 248, rue de Rivoli, 1st. Tel.: 42.60.37.97. One flight up. From 9:30 a.m. to 6:30 p.m.; closed Sunday. Weathered and irresistably old-fashioned. Service tends to be touch-and-go. Great for scones, apple pie, Christmas pudding, and of course, pure Ceylon tea.

*Angelina:* 226, rue de Rivoli, 1st. Tel.: 42.60.82.00. From 9:30 a.m. to 7 p.m., on Saturday and Sunday to 7:30 p.m. The showiness of Rumpelmeyer's and the snobbiest tea, well worth the long wait. The "Africain" pastry is always good, the Mont-blanc less consistently so.

*Le Meurice:* 228, rue de Rivoli, 1st. Tel.: 42.60.38.60. Opposite the reception desk. From 5 p.m. to dinnertime, every day. In the great French tradition, with chandeliers and gilt. Avoid the awful pastries. A pot of China tea is enough. Americans adore the place.

# Tea-Time Outdoors

*Ritz:* 15, place Vendôme, 1st. Tel.: 42.60.38.30. From 3 to 7 p.m., every day. Deluxe tea under the plane trees. Waiters in formal attire. Best pastries: the chocolate cake and the *mille-feuille.* A pot of Ceylon tea: 70 F.

*Jardin de Thé:* 10, rue Brise-Miche, 4th. Tel.: 42.74.35.26. Between Saint-Merri and the Pompidou Center. From 3 to 7:30 p.m. (until midnight in the summer); closed Tuesday. Sit and admire Tinguely's fountain on a hot day. Excellent teas; the tarts are better than the scones: 40 F.

*La Grande Cascade* and *L'Auberge du Bonheur:* bois de Boulogne, 16th. Tel.: 45.27.33.51 and 42.24.10.17. Near the rond-point de Longchamp. From 4 to 6 p.m. every day. The former is snobbish and disappointing; the latter calmer, with better service. Both offer mediocre pastries from the same kitchen. 50 F. and 38 F.

*Muscade:* 36, rue de Montpensier, 1st. Tel.: 42.97.51.36. Near Le Grand Vefour. Tea from 3 to 7 p.m. every day. Recommended only for the delightful Palais-Royal terrace. Forget the welcome; just have a cup of tea: 16 F.

# Tea and Shopping

*Ladurée: haute couture shopping.* 16, rue Royale, 8th. Tel.: 42.60.21.79. At the beginning of faubourg Saint-Honoré. From 8:30 a.m. to 7 p.m.; closed Sunday. Excellent croissants and chocolate macaroons. 40 F.

*Pandora: browsing in the old passages.* 24, passage Choiseul, 2nd. Tel.: 42.97.56.01. On rue des Petits-Champs, near the Banque Nationale de Paris. From noon to 7 p.m.; closed Saturday. Chocolate cake or prune cake. 40 F.

*Thé Cool: shopping on rue de Passy.* 10, rue Jean-Bologne, 16th. Tel.: 42.24.69.13. Opposite the church of Notre-Dame-de-Passy. Every day from noon to 7 p.m., from 11 a.m. on Sunday. Chocolate *marquise* (chocolate mousse cake) and scones. 30 F.

*Croque la Lune: the department store area.* 40, rue des Mathurins, 8th. Tel.: 42.65.18.05. Next to the Théâtre des Mathurins. From 11:30 a.m. to 8 p.m.; closed Sunday. Well-prepared, high quality tarts. 35 F.

For additional information on tea rooms, consult *Paris Sucré* (by the same author in collaboration with R. Girard, Hachette, 1986), from which these suggestions have been gleaned.

# Académie de Billard de Clichy-Montmartre

**7 p.m.**

Imagine a grand, ornate turn-of-the-century hall, in which a long row of billiard tables stand under glaring lights. The pros, dressed in black, play before a captivated audience. Cigarettes dangle from their lips; ashes fall to the floor. Engrossed in the proceedings, nobody even bothers to go for a drink at the bar. Only a few oldtimers, playing cards in a corner of the room, seem oblivious to what's going on.

You'll notice some people heading for the backroom; if you follow them, you'll discover an astonishing gambling den. A croupier presides over a game of "multicolore" (a kind of poor man's roulette), surrounded by a throng of cigarette-puffing, beer-quaffing players.

This game room is off-limits to women, military men, and minors, according to a sign on the wall. *Caveat emptor.*

- **With whom:** a snob, or a pool hustler.

- **Where:** 84, rue de Clichy, 9th. Tel.: 48.74.08.64. Can be seen from place Clichy. To get into the gambling room, ask one of the regulars to introduce you.

- **When:** from 1:30 to 11:30 p.m. (for billiards), until 3 a.m. for roulette. A good time to go is around 7 p.m.—but sometimes the billiards matches go on past midnight.

- **Recommended:** possibly a whisky.

- **Welcome:** nonexistent.

- **Dress:** like Paul Newman in *The Hustler.*

- **Bottom line:** observe the scene silently.

- **Cost:** 80 F.

- **Emergency alternative:** *Cockney Tavern*, 38 boulevard de Clichy, 9th. Tel.: 48.74.36.71. From noon to 4 a.m. A phony kind of pub, but anyway, it's a special British hideaway in Pigalle.

# Bar du Pont Royal

When it comes to bars, everyone has a favorite. The fashionable philosopher, Bernard-Henri Lévy, and his editors from Fayard go to the Twickenham. Writer Philippe Sollers and his cronies from Gallimard Press go to the wood-paneled Pont Royal, tucked away below street level, for a good chat. Comfortably installed in an armchair, you'll be tempted to carry on an erudite conversation, or better yet, to listen to your neighbors discuss the Goncourt Prize, copyrights, or "Apostrophes" (the weekly literary TV program).

Order a kir and ponder the plight of post-Modernism. Or soothe your writer's cramp with a dry martini. (In the old days, it would have been absinthe.)

The menu touts this place as "the literary bar of the Left Bank," but maintaining that reputation has been difficult since the departure of Francis, the bartender. He was the mentor and father-confessor of thirsty writers from the entire Saint-Germain area.

- **With whom:** Françoise Sagan or Norman Mailer.
- **Where:** 7, rue Montalembert, 7th. Tel.: 45.44.38.27. Between rue du Bac and rue de l'Université, next to the Hôtel Pont Royal.
- **When:** from 11 a.m. to 2 a.m.; closed Sunday. Lunch isn't bad here: haddock, for example, served on the low cocktail tables.
- **Recommended:** kir, dry martini, the Pont Royal cocktail.
- **Welcome:** self-important.
- **Dress:** strive for rakish charm; a bright wool muffler for men is *de rigueur.*
- **Bottom line:** intellectual eavesdropping.
- **Cost:** 40 F.
- **Emergency alternative:** *Le Twickenham,* 70, rue des Saints-Pères, 6th. Tel.: 42.22.96.85.

# Le Forum ♥

**7 p.m.**

It's seven o'clock. Happy hour. But the well-dressed executives have not come with their colleagues and they're not clustering around the bar. Instead, they prefer to sink alongside their lovers into the deep, plush club chairs that are oddly arranged in concentric circles on the leaf-patterned carpet.

The executives don't gaze into their lovers' eyes, but tap their fingers imperceptibly on the arms of their chairs while the huge, shiny jukeboxes spew out the foxtrots, jazz hits, and pop favorites of their youth.

The bossy bartender, who is nevertheless friendly and sincere, serves them an imported beer or a Festival cocktail, made with champagne, orange juice, and pear liqueur. Just one complaint: the only brand of champagne available is Lanson. They could surely do better than that.

- **With whom:** a perfectly proper lover.
- **Where:** 4, boulevard Malesherbes, 8th. Tel.: 42.65.37.86. Near the church of the Madeleine.
- **When:** from 11:30 a.m. to 2 a.m.; closed Saturday afternoon and Sunday.
- **Recommended:** the Festival cocktail, a Jack Collins.
- **Welcome:** status-conscious.
- **Dress:** come-as-you-are, straight from work.
- **Bottom line:** a respectable bar.
- **Cost:** 50 F.
- **Emergency alternative:** *Le Blue Fox Bar* (p. 68).

# Ledoyen

**7 p.m.**

Where can you go for a drink on the Champs-Élysées? The sole English pub has been replaced by a restaurant (the Bistrot de la Gare), Fouquet's terrace simply isn't what it used to be, and the other cafés are boring. So it's Ledoyen.

It's better to enter directly from the terrace, rather than tramp through all the dining rooms and have the maîtres d' inform you condescendingly, "The bar is in the other direction."

Often empty, this English-style place really can't afford to put on such airs. You'll enjoy it for the flowered vista, the quiet nooks, and—more prosaically —for the abundance of potato chips, olives, and salted almonds on the table.

- **With whom:** a doyen, or his parents.
- **Where:** at the carré of the Champs-Élysées, 8th. Tel.: 42.65.95.86. Coming from place de la Concorde, on the left-hand side of the avenue just before the Petit Palais.
- **When:** from 11 a.m. to midnight.
- **Recommended:** a kir, a fruit-juice cocktail.
- **Welcome:** ostentatious.
- **Dress:** Hermès accessories are advised.
- **Bottom line:** for a light apéritif; easy parking.
- **Cost:** 50 F.
- **Emergency alternative:** *Fouquet's*, for the terrace and the memories: 99, avenue des Champs-Élysées, 8th. Tel.: 47.23.70.60.

# Le Lloyds

**7 p.m.**     Delicious anachronism

This could be the captain's cabin, crammed with bucca-neers' pistols, smuggled ivory, African masks, Burmese Buddhas, votive objects, and hunting trophies from every port.

A faithful and ageless maître d'—like a valet who respectfully carries on the traditions of his dead master —sets the tables with spotless white cloths, offers a newspaper to his early customers, and personally and expertly prepares remarkable White Ladies and spicy Pink Ladies.

Conservative executives from the neighborhood don't really care for such fancy drinks, and are happy enough to down a pint of beer with their colleagues before going home to watch the eight o'clock news.

- o **With whom:** an acquaintance from l'Électricité de France, whose offices are nearby.
- o **Where:** 23, rue Treilhard, 8th. Tel.: 45.63.21.23. At the corner of avenue de Messine, on the side of rue de la Bienfaisance.
- o **When:** from noon to 9 p.m.; closed Saturday, Sunday, and holidays.
- o **Recommended:** the Pink and White Ladies, a Wild Turkey bourbon, an Americano (special house recipe).
- o **Welcome:** a bartender out of the books.
- o **Dress:** V.I.P.
- o **Bottom line:** a Parisian safari.
- o **Cost:** 25 F.
- o **Emergency alternative:** *Le Forum* (p. 101).

# La Palette

Saint-Germain
Artistic

La Palette still attracts a sizable crowd. As if to provoke you, bad paintings "in the manner of" so-and-so are conspicuously hung on the walls: an overdone Impressionistic belltower, a Cubist still-life, a Utrillo-ish view of Montmartre.

The artistic clientele, from the Beaux-Arts and other art schools, sit on the terrace, beat a path to the bar, or settle down in the billiard-less billiard room. They love to listen in on the ethereal conversations of their narcissistic neighbors, who are admiring themselves in the big mirrors under the tolerant, kindly eye of the waiters depicted on the tile murals.

As for the bearded boss, an affectedly gruff guy, he'll serve you a mediocre kir or a glass of red wine that you could use on a salad, and a platter of finely sliced ham canapés. Just try to ask him for a glass of tapwater. . . .

- o **With whom:** an up-and-coming artist.
- o **Where:** 43, rue de Seine, 6th. Tel.: 43.26.68.15. Near the École des Beaux-Arts.
- o **When:** every day but Sunday, from 8 a.m. to 2 a.m.
- o **Recommended:** the kir.
- o **Welcome:** aggressive.
- o **Dress:** artistic.
- o **Bottom line:** go for the ambience, the terrace, the neighborhood.
- o **Cost:** 15 F. for a kir.
- o **Emergency alternative:** the bar of l'Hôtel, *Le Belier* (p. 190).

# Le Tribulum

Messy, unpredictable, and preposterous, Le Tribulum should be visited in the same spirit as you would a museum of kitsch, a weird surrealistic environment, or a Transcendental Meditation meeting room. Go with a like-minded friend. The walls are covered with metaphysical slogans and Tarot cards, the tables have explanations of "the functional hypotheses of clairvoyance," and the main room is cluttered with allegorical pictures of the zodiac and unsavory objects for divination, all of it hidden from the street by bead curtains.

If this bazaar leaves you cold, try the crypt under the starry ceiling. Enthroned between the wings of a dove, you'll gulp down some sinister-looking ice cream or an astrological cocktail under the stare of a plaster *Thinker*.

According to a poster, "every Thursday evening Le Tribulum invites you to participate in the spiritual séance entitled: Witnessing the Irrational."

- **With whom:** a psychic friend.
- **Where:** 62, rue Saint-Denis, 1st. Tel.: 42.36.01.01. Impossible to miss: follow the pedestrian street.
- **When:** every day from 8 a.m. to 2 a.m. A secluded terrace is open in the summer.
- **Recommended:** beware of the astrological cocktails; the Geminis are luckier than the Cancers.
- **Welcome:** other-worldly.
- **Dress:** any deviation will be analyzed.
- **Bottom line:** must be seen with the third eye.
- **Cost:** 38 F.
- **Emergency alternative:** *Café Costes* (pp. 12, 182).

# Discreet Hotels:  ♥
## Le Warwick, Le Raphaël,
## Le Normandy, Le Lenox

Off the beaten path and yet centrally located, slightly pretentious but well maintained, these comfortable hotels are geared more to visitors from the provinces than to urbane Parisians.

Here, in an atmosphere of anonymity and discretion, you can meet the headhunter who wants to check you out, the married woman who needs to speak to you urgently, or the business associate you want to thank for a favor.

*Le Warwick:* 5, rue de Berri, 8th. Tel.: 45.63.14.11. Every day from 11 a.m. to 2 a.m. Of special interest: behind the bar there's a salon that's completely hidden away. Have a whisky served with stuffed olives, chorizo, and peanuts. 50 F.

*Le Raphaël:* 17, avenue Kléber, 16th. Tel.: 45.02.16.00. Every day from 11 a.m. to 10 p.m. Of special interest: a neo-Gothic décor, comfortable club chairs. An ageless bartender will suggest having a "Turner" cocktail, to match the painting over the cash register. 50 F.

*Le Normandy:* 7, rue de l'Échelle, 1st. Tel.: 42.60.30.21. From 11 a.m. to midnight; closed Saturday and on Sunday afternoon. Of special interest: a hop away from rue de Rivoli, a very British atmosphere. Try the house cocktail, made with bourbon and Benedictine brandy. 45 F.

*Le Lenox:* 9, rue de l'Université, 7th. Tel.: 42.96.10.95. Every day from 5 p.m. to 2 a.m. Of special interest: behind the Italian blinds, literary intrigues take place. Good selection of whiskey and mixed drinks made with champagne. 40 F.

Evening

*Offbeat Dinners*
*Romantic Dinners*
*Dinners for Special*
*Occasions*
*Fashionable Dinners*

# The Chicago Pizza Pie
# Factory

**8 p.m.**

If you're homesick for the Great Lakes, miss your old college campus, or need a fast-food fix, head for the Parisian version of the Chicago Pizza Pie Factory.

Meet at the Loop-shaped bar, so you can kibbitz about the last baseball or football games while Chicago radio station WBBM blares in the background. A squeaky-clean hostess with a frozen smile will take you to your table, which might be designated State Navy Pier or Lake Shore Drive.

In this aluminum and red plastic garage, you're sure to like the tasty, authentic deep-dish pizzas, the crisp garlic bread, and the salad topped with Thousand Island dressing.

Sinatra was right: "Chicago is my kind of town."

o **With whom:** homesick Chicagoans and any up-rooted Americans.

o **Where:** 5, rue de Berri, 8th. Tel.: 45.62.50.23. Right off the Champs-Élysées, in a former garage.

o **When:** every day from noon to 1 a.m.

o **Recommended:** deep-dish pizza with pepperoni, Thousand Island salad, "Chicago cake."

o **Welcome:** ordinary.

o **Dress:** blue jeans compulsory.

o **Bottom line:** Yankee Come Home—after an 8 or 10 p.m. movie.

o **Cost:** 80 F.

o **Emergency alternative:** *City Rock Café*, 13, rue de Berri, 8th. Tel.: 43.59.52.09. A rock supermarket, with teeny-boppers, huge hamburgers, and sometimes France's own Johnny Halliday. Every day from noon to 2:30 a.m.

# Chinatown Olympiades

8 p.m.

Chinatown
Gaudy

The Olympiades puts on the airs of a Chinese palace, with scores of tables lined up under phony Delft chandeliers, as if expecting the arrival of high dignitaries. Murals depict a dozen young girls combing their hair, dancing, and praying among a thousand stylized flowers and rocks—a saccharin illustration of *Dream of the Red House.*

Chinese families like to hold their banquets and family parties here, helping themselves to the Cantonese dishes, the steamed dim sum, and the roasted meat hanging at the entrance. Bustling around with the impeccable maîtres d' are cooks in thongs, pushing shopping carts that they've borrowed from the supermarket downstairs. The Chinese idea of luxury doesn't exclude doing the cooking and dishwashing right in the dining room.

- **With whom:** a bunch of friends who have been to Hong Kong or Taipei.
- **Where:** 44, avenue d'Ivry, 13th. Tel.: 45.84.72.21. An immense restaurant above a shopping mall.
- **When:** every day from noon to 3 p.m. and 7 to 11 p.m.
- **Recommended:** Chinese soup or shrimp wontons, Shanghai beef or rainbow lacquered duck, little coconut tarts.
- **Welcome:** formal but not stiff.
- **Dress:** anything goes.
- **Bottom line:** exciting Chinese cuisine.
- **Cost:** 52 F. for the fixed menu, 150 F. to indulge à la carte.
- **Emergency alternative:** there's plenty to choose from in the neighborhood: *Hawaï*, 87, avenue d'Ivry. Tel.: 45.86.91.90. Draws the entire Vietnamese population of Paris for its incomparable *phos* and *nems*. There's no service charge, and you'll understand why: the waiters are so fast they don't even give you time to empty your bowl. 80 F. Closed Thursday.

# Le Baalbeck                                    ♥

## 9 p.m.

A nondescript place in a deserted neighborhood. Hardly a Lebanese flag or any reminder of Baalbeck to stir your memories. Of course, there are all sorts of those famous Middle Eastern hors d'oeuvres called *mezze:* tabouleh, various vegetables, and lamb cooked every which way.

Suddenly, with an ear-splitting din (the sound system has been turned up a bit too high), a fabulous creature makes her entrance. Swaying to the enthusiastic applause of the customers, she looks around for a victim.

And in a minute she's beside you, wrapping herself around your chair. So persistent is she that finally, dizzy from the sight of her undulating belly, you slip the bill she's been waiting for into a safe nook. Your cronies at the table are thrilled.

o **With whom:** a bunch of merry-makers.

o **Where:** 16, rue de Mazagran, 10th. Tel.: 47.70.70.02. At the corner of rue de l'Echiquier. Don't sit on the dining room side.

o **When:** from noon to 3 p.m. and, for the belly-dancing, from 8 p.m. to midnight; closed Sunday.

o **Recommended:** ask for the *mezze*—you'll get dozens of them.

o **Welcome:** cold at first, then warmer and warmer.

o **Dress:** décolletée.

o **Bottom line:** belly-dancing as you never dared imagine it.

o **Cost:** 150 F. maximum.

o **Emergency alternative:** *Julien* (p. 178).

# Carr's                                  ♥

## 9 p.m.                                  Ireland in song

Far from the moors of his native Donegal, in a neighbor-hood that's deserted right after office hours, a deter-mined Irishman has decided, against all odds, to replicate a real "singing pub."

The empty front room discourages passersby, per-haps intentionally. For only the true sons and daughters of Erin crowd into the backroom, which touts the splendors of Ireland and the owner's village in particu-lar.

The owner, Carr, is the soul of the place, personally welcoming his tweedy friends and serving them nation-al dishes like beech-smoked wild salmon flown in by Aer Lingus. He can't help but interrupt his serving to play whatever ballad pops into his head and everyone joins in: one pulls a flute out of his pocket, another picks up a guitar, while you sink slowly into a deep melancholy.

- ○ **With whom:** a friend from the old sod.
- ○ **Where:** 18, rue Thérèse, 1st. Tel.: 42.96.04.29. Between rue Sainte-Anne and avenue de l'Opéra.
- ○ **When:** From noon to 2:30 p.m. and 7:30 to 11 p.m., sometimes later, if the mood so dictates. Especially lively on weekends.
- ○ **Recommended:** wild salmon, bacon and cabbage, leg of lamb with mint sauce, rhubarb pie, Irish coffee. And Guinness.
- ○ **Welcome:** very warm.
- ○ **Dress:** go native.
- ○ **Bottom line:** back to the moors.
- ○ **Cost:** 150 F.
- ○ **Emergency alternative:** *Les Boucholeurs* (p. 132).

# Le Dogon

*République*
Refinement

There are no Dogon masks or tom-toms evoking images of the jungle in this discreet restaurant. No folklore here.

Nor will you find rastas, immigrants, and other fashionable rebels, but instead, beautiful women in flowing African boubous and evening gowns, immaculate diplomats, and dignitaries wearing huge rings, heavy watches, and wide ties.

Le Dogon isn't sectarian: the cuisine is a happy blend of dishes from Senegal, Cameroon, and Benin, with some South Sea island touches, while the music is predominantly from Mali.

Elegant women don't mind coming here alone. They don't remain alone very long because it's so easy to strike up a conversation with someone.

- **With whom:** some friends you want to fool around with.
- **Where:** 30, rue René-Boulanger, 10th. Tel.: 42.41.95.85. A little street linking place de la République to the main boulevards.
- **When:** from 8:30 p.m. to about 3 a.m.; closed Monday.
- **Recommended:** crab stuffed with soya, lamb brochettes, Yanah (chicken marinated in lemon) or N'dole, the Dogon coupe (ice cream); red Bandol (wine).
- **Welcome:** refined and attentive.
- **Dress:** what the hell—get all dolled up.
- **Bottom line:** an eye-opener—and possibly an encounter.
- **Cost:** 180 F.
- **Emergency alternative:** *Fouta Toro*, 3, rue du Nord, 18th. Tel: 42.55.42.73. An excellent maffé (chicken or beef in a peanut sauce) for 50 F., jammed into a friendly honky-tonk place.

# *Farafina*

*Far East*
Easy-going

Never, if you searched for years, could you find a more carefree African restaurant in Paris. Black musicians record here for Radio Tchatch, the city's African radio station. In vain, the owner of the place asks them to keep the volume down. The waiters hang around the band, chatting. They forget about your order. And the checks get mixed up.

But you'll be charmed by the spontaneous atmosphere. The musicians really are the best African musicians in Paris, and the braised half chicken makes the long wait worth it. "But why are you all in such a hurry?" they say.

Indeed, why not take this opportunity to cool out a bit, to chat with your roving neighbors, and dance among the tables while you're waiting to appease your hunger?

- o **With whom:** a journalist from *Actuel* magazine.
- o **Where:** 12, rue Quincampoix, 4th. Tel.: 48.04.-50.52.
- o **When:** from 8 p.m. to 1:15 a.m. (take your time); closed Monday.
- o **Recommended:** braised chicken or couscous with millet. Ginger digestive to finish.
- o **Welcome:** cheerful.
- o **Dress:** like a weary newspaper columnist: safari jacket and sneakers.
- o **Bottom line:** to get in touch with Africa.
- o **Cost:** 120 F.
- o **Emergency alternative:** in the same style, *Le Petit Chartier* is interesting. 16, rue Jules-Verne, 11th. Tel.: 43.55.36.35. Near the Bellcville district. It's not expensive, it's relatively good, but it's like eating in Bamako: 80 F.

# *Haynes* ♥

Haynes has a tough pioneer spirit and deep Cajun roots. It looks like a log cabin on the outside, a thatched cottage at the bar, a dive in the dining room.

The rough walls seem to be carved out of rock, the twisted columns seem to be coiled around each other, and the candles shed a nostalgic light on owner Leroy's souvenirs: stills from boxing matches and films he appeared in, as well as signed photos from his friends in the jazz and entertainment worlds.

Leroy is a jolly giant of a man—a real scrapper, a down-home character, who personally serves you native American dishes, made according to his recipes. After a scorching-hot chili con carne or some impressive New Orleans gumbo, you'll be less eager to tackle the banana or apple pie—which will, in fact, be disappointing.

Haynes is *the* top American restaurant in Paris. Its name is confidentially passed around among the big names of Hollywood, as well as among Parisians. Don't give away the secret. . . .

- **With whom:** a French friend you want to impress.
- **Where:** 3, rue Clauzel, 9th. Tel.: 48.78.40.63. Starting from place Gustave-Thoudouze, head toward rue Pigalle.
- **Recommended:** New Orleans gumbo or chili con carne, coconut pie.
- **Not recommended:** apple pie, chicken with honey, banana or lemon pie.
- **Welcome:** friendly, but Haynes is often in hiding.
- **Dress:** jeans and loafers.
- **Bottom line:** a touch of Americana for a lovers' tryst.
- **Cost:** 150 F.
- **Emergency alternative:** *Anarkali*, 4, place Gustave-Toudouze, 9th. Tel.: 48.78.39.84. At the end of rue Clauzel. Curry and tandooris with the locals. 100 F.

# Le Paprika ♥

*Near the Jardin des Plantes*
Gypsy

At first glance, nothing catches your attention in this neighborhood hash-house, whose stuccoed walls are carefully covered with souvenirs of the homeland—except owner Czeko Laszlo, who impresses you with his noble bearing and his intensity.

Listen to him expound on the merits of Hungarian cuisine, which uses lots of paprika and other Ottoman spices. As he tells it, Hungary is the land of origin of foie gras and also of Tokay wine—an elixir of kings that was jealously guarded by a whole regiment of Cossacks at the court of Catherine the Great.

Your meal will be sumptuous and sparkling, and you'll be serenaded by a gypsy trio just as Prince Esterhazy was.

- **With whom:** a hard-to-get woman.
- **Where:** 43, rue Poliveau, 5th. Tel.: 43.31.65.86. A stone's throw from the mosque, toward the Austerlitz Station.
- **When:** at noon, and every evening from 9 p.m. until at least midnight; closed Sunday.
- **Recommended:** escalope of foie gras or young goat cheese with cumin, the Hungarian sampler, strudel.
- **Welcome:** rather grand, but still family style.
- **Dress:** discreetly seductive.
- **Bottom line:** sobbing violins . . . culturally authentic.
- **Cost:** 250 F.
- **Emergency alternative:** *Polidor* (p. 36).

# Sapna

**9 p.m.**

A handsome Sikh in a white turban stands guard. A thousand stars twinkle on the ceiling. A rose decorates each table. And yet you're in a bistro seating about 20 people that is furnished in pure imitation Louis XVI.

Silly? No, charming. Because you'll rarely be received as kindly as you will by Kahtri, a native of Punjab—a descendant of kings and warriors—and by his companion, a Moroccan woman who wears a sari.

This is Kahtri's second restaurant. He makes excellent tandoori dishes, and an equally good lamb knuckle with 24 spices. "Hope" ("Aasha," the name of his first place) has turned into a "dream" ("Sapna" in Indian). He deserves it.

- o **With whom:** a long-lost friend.
- o **Where:** 160, rue de Charenton, place du Colonel-Bourgoin, 12th. Tel.: 43.46.73.33. At the end of rue de Charenton, past boulevard Diderot.
- o **When:** from noon to 2 p.m. and 7:30 to 11 p.m.; closed on Saturday at lunchtime, and Monday.
- o **Recommended:** lamb knuckle marinated in 24 spices (barrah kebab), butter chicken, Indian bread (cheese nam), saffron rice, and nothing more.
- o **Welcome:** effusive.
- o **Dress:** elegant, but casual.
- o **Cost:** 100 F. at noon, 140 F. in the evening.
- o **Emergency alternative:** *Aasha*, the first place, at 18, rue Greneta, 2nd. Tel.: 42.36.71.55. The same tandoori dishes served in a cellar in les Halles.

# Le Studio

**9 p.m.**

Tex-Mex restaurants thrive in Paris. Le Studio continues to draw a big crowd despite the success of its rival, *Café Pacifico*.

Le Studio is located in a private house that is also home to a dancing school, and from the inner courtyard windows you can see (and hear) a mélange of ballet, tap, and American rock.

It is meant to look like a western-style saloon, with a painted backdrop that resembles Carson City, photos of Buffalo Bill and Geronimo, Indian rugs, and sombreros. Instead of outlaws, you'll find outlanders (mainly from America) who come here to dip tortilla chips in hot sauce, outdrink each other with tequila, and fortify themselves with "deluxe Mexican plates." They joke around with the waiters and waitresses—good-looking guys and sexy gals—all on a first-name basis. "Just call me Al."

- **With whom:** man-to-man, to talk about women.
- **Where:** 41, rue du Temple, 4th. Tel.: 42.74.10.38. In the courtyard of the Café de la Gare opposite the dancing school. When you arrive, give your first name to the waitress, who will put you on the list to be seated.
- **When:** from 7 p.m. to 12:30 a.m.
- **Recommended:** the deluxe Mexican plate, coconut sorbet, and tequila. The complete menu is okay too, and includes a good guacamole. And, recently introduced—a good barbecue.
- **Welcome:** fresh and young.
- **Dress:** Wild West.
- **Bottom line:** an amusing scene, America-in-Paris; and the courtyard is nice in the summer.
- **Cost:** 120 F.
- **Emergency alternative:** *l'Aviatic* (p. 180).

# L'Absinthe ♥

Marché Saint-Honoré
A *la* Proust

♈ ♈ ♈

This feminine and flowery turn-of-the-century restaurant evokes the pleasant effects of anisette rather than the evil ones of absinthe. It's more Lewis Carroll than Edgar Allen Poe. The bourgeois-style dining room upstairs looks like the comfortable domicile of a well-bred young woman—slightly cluttered but well intentioned —with the incongruous addition of a painted ceiling retrieved from a bakery.

Young couples prefer the winter garden setting, with curtain fabrics swirling with palm leaves and the banquettes upholstered with orchids. Dedicated to the female ideal, the room shamelessly displays ondines, Ophelias, nymphs, and portraits of great ladies.

Charming waiters serve dishes that are elegant, inventive, and sometimes brilliant, such as the coquilles Saint-Jacques with a fennel sauce.

- **With whom:** as a couple.
- **Where:** 24, place du Marché-Saint-Honoré, 1st. Tel.: 42.60.02.45. The east side of the square. Ask for the winter garden.
- **When:** from 12:30 to 2:30 p.m. and 8 to 11:30 p.m.; closed Saturday and Sunday.
- **Recommended:** terrine of leeks with truffle, baked lotte with pink pepper, partly cooked foie gras.
- **Welcome:** charming.
- **Dress:** elaborate.
- **Bottom line:** a seductive setting.
- **Cost:** 230 F.
- **Emergency alternative:** *Willi's* (p. 75).

# *Beauvilliers*

**9 p.m.**

Montmartre
Elegant

Never has a Parisian restaurant succeeded so well in cultivating a festive air. The terraces stretch out along the steps of the Butte Montmartre, bordered by flowering hortensias that would do justice to the Piazza di Spagna in Rome.

Inside, large bouquets on pedestals add allure to the suite of fashionable rooms: the flower-show salon that lovingly displays wedding bouquets under glass; the Boilly salon with original charcoal drawings; and the windmill salon, named after a windmill that is no longer there, except in the owner's memory.

Edouard Carlier is lord of this manor and a grand alderman of the Montmartre guilds. He knows exactly how to add a royal luster to your romantic dinners. You can be sure your companion will be charmed by the attentive service, by the delicacy of the old-fashioned or nouvelle dishes, and by your boundless generosity.

- **With whom:** a great lady.
- **Where:** 52, rue Lamarck, 18th. Tel.: 42.54.54.42. Behind the Butte, following rue Caulaincourt: first right after avenue Junot.
- **When:** from noon to 3 p.m. and 7:30 to 10:30 p.m. The terrace is besieged in good weather. But be careful—the standard slips when the boss is away.
- **Recommended:** fresh artichoke bottoms topped with crab chiffonnade, lamb brains deglazed with Xeres vinegar, Morgon.
- **Not recommended:** veal kidneys with pistachio and marsala cream sauce.
- **Welcome:** overwhelming and attentive.
- **Dress:** "I love what you're wearing; it's so silky."
- **Bottom line:** for courtship, in a courtly style.
- **Cost:** 400 F.
- **Emergency alternative:** *Les Fusains* (p. 138).

# Le Bougnat ♥

## 9 p.m.

This Auvergnat-style restaurant is highly civilized. At one time it was the favorite meeting place of French President Georges Pompidou, a great patron of the arts, who came here to chat with his friends from the nearby art galleries. It was like a salon for the habitués of Saint-Germain-des-Prés.

Today, though, the customers are more likely to be pop singers, new faces in French cinema, and fashion models, and the conversation is less of existentialism and more of the entertainment industry.

This self-satisfied, bustling little world may amuse your girlfriend. She'll certainly like the aesthetic interior, where every armchair, every candlestick, is a little treasure—the gift of a knowing friend, a flea market "find," or a collector's item.

- **With whom:** a would-be Parisienne.
- **Where:** 15, rue Séguier, 6th. Tel.: 43.54.31.55. Between rue Saint-André-des-Arts and the Seine.
- **When:** from 8 p.m. to midnight; closed Sunday.
- **Recommended:** raw salmon with dill, magret of duck with Xeres vinegar and a fruit purée, warm mango tart; red Bouzy.
- **Not recommended:** stuffed cabbage and other house specialties: too heavy.
- **Welcome:** clubby.
- **Dress:** Ungaro.
- **Bottom line:** just like home, dear.
- **Cost:** 250 F.; fixed menu at 170 F.
- **Emergency alternative:** *Castel*, 15, rue Princesse, 6th. Tel.: 43.26.90.22. *The* private club in Paris. Bring your credentials and try to get in.

# Île de Kashmir ♥

## 9 p.m.

A marble fountain, walls hung with Kashmiri fabric, fretwork screens, highly refined service—all this is designed to re-create the glory of the mythical garden of Shalimar, the hymn to beauty of an 17th-century emperor-poet.

But the clientele hardly notices the scholarly allusions of this floating palace. In fact, why bother to offer them the whole range of Indian culinary creations when their thoughts are so obviously elsewhere?

For only *couples* venture onto this houseboat, cozying up to each other on the comfortable banquettes, letting themselves be transported by the haunting music, and enjoying a breathtaking view of half the Eiffel Tower.

- **With whom:** an Indian lover.
- **Where:** quai Debilly, opposite 32, avenue de New York, 16th. Tel.: 47.23.50.97. Under the footbridge at the quai Branly. Plenty of parking.
- **When:** from 12:30 to 2:30 p.m. and 7:30 to 11 p.m.
- **Recommended:** Malabar crab, Bhuna lamb chop, mango kulfi (Indian version of ice cream). In fact, just follow your instincts.
- **Welcome:** attentive and discreet.
- **Dress:** flirtatious.
- **Cost:** 250 F.
- **Emergency alternative:** if only to be on the water, try the houseboat alongside, *Le Shogun*, practically the exclusive domain of Japanese tourists. Also on the quai Debilly. Tel.: 47.20.05.04.

# Le Jules Verne ♥

*Eiffel Tower*
Jules Verne's place

## Rendez-vous Award of the Year

If you've always dreamt of the Phantom of the Opera, of Quasimodo of Notre-Dame, or of ghosts at the Louvre, wait no longer: make a nighttime foray up the secret staircase of the Eiffel Tower, tell the guard you've reserved a table, and take the hidden elevator up to the Jules Verne restaurant, tucked away on the second floor.

This space could well be one of those secret passages that, according to popular legend, are believed to exist in every special monument. Or simply the loft of Gustave Eiffel, deliberately painted black to provide a backdrop to the city lights below, and furnished in metal to echo the surrounding girders.

Night falls around you. And, bathed in the light of the tower, you can gaze at Paris, which seems to have come under the magic spell of filmmaker René Clair.

- **With whom:** a passionate partner.
- **Where:** the Eiffel Tower, Paris, France. Tel.: 45.55.61.44. The tower's south pillar; special elevator to the second floor. An attendant will park your Bugatti.
- **When:** Every day until 11 p.m. Reserve two weeks in advance. If space is available, you may be able to have a drink at the bar between 10 and 11 p.m.
- **Recommended:** the superb beech-smoked salmon, roast grouse with green cabbage (a rare bird in Paris), and the Jules Verne dessert. Champagne, of course.
- **Welcome:** impeccable, under the direction of Monsieur Robert.
- **Dress:** black.
- **Bottom line:** inspiring.
- **Cost:** 500 F.; 220 F. for the amazing luncheon menu that includes cheese and dessert.

- **Emergency alternative:** to see the tower, *Le Toit de Passy*, 94, avenue Paul-Doumer, 16th. Tel.: 45.24.55.37. A sumptuous menu for 365 F., albeit without the fantasy.

# Maison de l'Amérique Latine ♥

**9 p.m.**

How wonderfully ironic: dining by candlelight in a French garden at the Varangeville mansion, which was designed for a king, and all thanks to the efforts of Régis Debray, the left-wing advisor to President Mitterrand, who decided to "democratize" this once-private club by opening it up to everyone.

Imagine a five-acre park in the heart of Saint-Germain, with a rose garden and chestnut trees. Set out some tables on the terrace. Add some candles and orchids. Sprinkle with some ambassadors and Parisian VIPs. And you'll have the most dazzling stage set of the summer.

However, if it rains you'll have to withdraw to a high-ceilinged but very small salon, which is a far cry from the extravagant folly of the spacious park.

- **With whom:** a marquis or marquise.
- **Where:** 217, boulevard Saint-Germain, 7th. Tel.: 45.49.33.23. Go straight through the Latin American cultural center and insist on a table in the garden.
- **When:** from noon to 2:30 p.m. and 8 to 10 p.m.; closed Saturday and Sunday.
- **Recommended:** order the simplest items: *pavé* of calves' liver, coffee parfait.
- **Not recommended:** the puff pastry dishes.
- **Welcome:** very Left Bank Saint-Germain.
- **Dress:** rustic.
- **Bottom line:** a romantic romp in the park.
- **Cost:** at least 250 F.
- **Emergency alternative:** *L'Oeillade*, 10, rue Saint-Simon, 7th. Tel.: 42.22.01.60. Family-style cuisine, a table d'hôte menu, a rustic ambience (but not overdone), and moderate prices (120 F.). The ideal place to be incognito.

# La Maison du Caviar   ♥

## 9 p.m.

La Maison du Caviar has rendered untold service to a whole generation of would-be seducers from the world of the theater, politics, and the media by following a set routine: a lengthy wait at the bar (except for the favored few), cramped seating that forces you to brush (if not actually rub) legs, blinis with salmon (if you're broke) or with caviar (if you're showing off), and vodka all around.

The handsome old gents from Saint-Moritz had high hopes when their dear little Maison took over the ailing Safari Club (see below), with its fake Thai waiters, its artificial flowers, and its decrepit armchairs. But the miracle didn't happen—the aging club hasn't even had a facelift.

- **With whom:** a showgirl from the Lido.
- **Where:** 21, rue Quentin-Bauchart, 8th. Tel.: 47.23.53.43. Off avenue George-V, near the Champs-Élysées.
- **When:** every day from 11:30 a.m. to 1 a.m.
- **Recommended:** zakouskis (hors d'oeuvres), blinis with salmon, nut cake; vodka.
- **Welcome:** bustling, but basically affable.
- **Dress:** expensive.
- **Bottom line:** sumptuous.
- **Cost:** 200 F. Much more if you can afford it.
- **Emergency alternative:** the annex, *Safari Club*, 3, avenue Matignon, 8th. Tel.: 43.59.51.48. From 2 p.m. to 2 a.m. The kingdom of kitsch, fairly amusing, and with intimate little nooks.

# Chez Marie ♥

Marie, formerly of Megève, the swank French ski resort, is now with Chez Marie in Paris. This delights the senators and Left Bank publishers who patronize the place at noon, and the actresses from the neighborhood who come in the evening (Catherine Deneuve, Marie-France Pisier, etc.), as well as the leading men-about-town.

Amid this Parisian bustle, the old bistro hasn't changed a bit: the zinc bar positively glowing with glasses of red wine, the now-graying mirror, and the souvenirs of yesteryear (like the poster for Cusenier absinthe that states it's "good for your health").

Sweet and charming Marie seats you graciously. Her old-fashioned cooking whets your appetite, and the candlelight makes you glow. You can't help but feel great.

- **With whom:** a senator, a publisher, a Don Juan? Up to you to decide.
- **Where:** 25, rue Servadoni, 6th. Tel.: 46.33.12.06. At the corner of rue Vaugirard, in front of the Luxembourg Palace.
- **When:** from noon to 2:30 p.m. and 8 to 10:30 p.m.; closed Saturday at noon and all day Sunday.
- **Recommended:** *beuchelle* of kidneys and sweetbreads or coquilles Saint-Jacques with watercress mousse, and especially, the iced mousse with nuts.
- **Welcome:** delightful.
- **Bottom line:** for quiet conversation.
- **Cost:** 200 F. At noon, a fixed menu at 110 F.
- **Emergency alternative:** *La Closerie des Lilas*, to catch a glimpse of some literary lions, if you like that sort of thing. 171, boulevard Montparnasse, 14th. Tel.: 43.26.70.50. Figure at least 300 F.

# *Maxim's*  ♥

## 9 p.m.

*Concorde*
Still magical

Don't shoot the piano player: all the customers at Maxim's are in seventh heaven. Risking everything for one night, they've planned down to the last detail: the formal tux and Madame's evening gown, caviar and buckets of champagne, serenades at the table, and foxtrots after dinner.

The fantastic décor fulfills their wildest dreams of the *Orient Express.* The extravagant prices give them a sense of power. And the ceremonious service imbues them with respect for the institution.

The most experienced diners will seek out Albert among the gang of maîtres d'; will spot the three "professionals" among the ingénues accompanying some aging industrialists; and will distinguish regulars from the tourists, who are raving about "Fraynce." All will be dazzled, and will rave about their "night at Maxim's" when they return home.

- **With whom:** a rich, if slightly long in the tooth, heiress.

- **Where:** 3, rue Royale, 8th. Tel.: 42.65.27.94. Look around—it's hard to miss.

- **When:** from 12:30 to 2:30 p.m. and 7:30 p.m. to 1 a.m. Formal dress required Friday evening. Closed Sunday in July and August.

- **Recommended:** instead of caviar, lobster, and other fancies, try the seafood crêpes, saddle of lamb, and nougat ice cream.

- **Not recommended:** the *feuilleté* of lobster with fresh morels, and the crayfish tails that are smothered under cabbage.

- **Welcome:** flamboyant.

- **Dress:** black tie compulsory Friday evening; other times, just an ordinary tie is required (unless you're Bruce Springsteen).

- **Bottom line:** at least once in your life.
- **Cost:** 800 F. maximum, without going crazy.
- **Emergency alternative:** close by . . . *Lucas-Carton* (p. 50).

# La Truffière ♥

## 9 p.m.

Secret trysts in suburban inns are a thing of the past; these days, you can carry on your romance at a picture-perfect manor house in the shadow of the Panthéon at La Truffière.

Ensconced on a sofa by the fireside, sip a kir royal next to the curled-up cat. You'll be joined by the cordial owner who will discuss the menu with you.

Naturally, the dining room has candles, old beams, and strains of Vivaldi in the background. The Périgord cuisine has pretty much disappeared since the recent change in ownership; the menu lists some ambitious culinary feats, but settles down to earth with such basic dishes as foie gras and *confit* of duck.

After sharing a *puits d'amour* (a luscious apple tart), return to the hearth. The restaurant empties out and you can start talking about serious things together.

- **With whom:** your latest love.
- **Where:** 4, rue Blainville, 5th. Tel.: 46.33.29.82. A short hop away from Contrescarpe; *don't* dine downstairs in the cellar.
- **When:** from noon to 2 p.m. and 7 to 10:30 p.m.; closed Monday.
- **Recommended:** foie gras sautéed in armagnac, *confit* of duck, *puits d'amour.*
- **Welcome:** well-meaning, but a little stiff.
- **Dress:** seductive.
- **Bottom line:** a perfect setting for seduction.
- **Cost:** 250 F. Fixed menu at 125 F.
- **Emergency alternative:** *Le Berthoud* (p. 131).

# Les Innocents ♥

9 p.m.

In spite of appearances and in spite of its name, Les Innocents is not a licensed brothel.

And yet, everything seems designed to ensure close encounters: set back at the end of a blind alley in a respectable neighborhood, hidden from onlookers by a heavy door that seems to require a password to open, it guarantees secrecy. The candles, dark corners, and old beams create a lusty *Tom Jones* ambience. And the tolerant and understanding maître d' seats consenting couples side by side on a narrow sofa.

You may find the approach a bit heavy-handed and think this club is all show. Don't knock it. The cuisine is perfect for someone who wants to make an impression and can pay for it. And Les Innocents keeps on delivering.

- **With whom:** a sex object.
- **Where:** 6, rue Robert-Estienne, 8th. Tel.: 43.59.40.70. At the back of the blind alley.
- **When:** from noon to 2:30 p.m. and 8 p.m. to 1 a.m.; closed Saturday at noon and all day Sunday.
- **Recommended:** kidneys with mustard, chocolat *fondant* (fudgy mousse).
- **Welcome:** like a private club.
- **Dress:** à la Saint-Moritz.
- **Bottom line:** for exchanging confidences.
- **Cost:** 220 F.
- **Emergency alternative:** *La Maison du Caviar* (p. 125).

# Le Berthoud

This place is like a dear grandmother who is perpetually surprising you. Her latest duplex, on Montagne Saint-Genevieve, is ultra-chic.

A sentimental soul, she adores her threadbare carpet, her Renaissance-inspired tapestries, and her hanging lamps.

But at the same time, she insists on hanging the premier poster of *Children of Paradise* and various lithographs that she considers avant-garde.

She's daring, too—she serves a hearty portion of raw chopped beef in a pot-au-feu broth, and follows that with a "mademoiselle's thigh"—"a fine flaky pastry caressed with virgin honey and crème fraîche," she explains slyly.

But like all grandmas, she tends to be overly generous. So order just one dish.

- **With whom:** someone between 30 and 35 years old.
- **Where:** 1, rue Valette, 5th. Tel.: 43.54.38.81. Down from the Panthéon, at the corner of rue Lanneau.
- **When:** from noon to 2 p.m. and 7 p.m. to 12:30 a.m.; closed Saturday at noon and all day Sunday.
- **Recommended:** one dish—quenelles or pot-au-feu —and a "mademoiselle's thigh."
- **Welcome:** theatrical, sometimes temperamental.
- **Dress:** an ascot rather than a tie.
- **Bottom line:** to talk over marital problems with your spouse.
- **Cost:** 200 F.
- **Emergency alternative:** *Le Petit Prince* (p. 176).

# Les Boucholeurs

**9 p.m.**

This fisherman's cottage is managed by two dynamic brothers-in-law who talk passionately about their mussel beds, display nautical paraphernalia on the walls, and prepare their mussels with a rare expertise. In fact, Les Boucholeurs follows the rhythm of the mussels market, closing only during the mussel reproduction season.

You can have mussels in a salad or in a "mouclade" (a curry-flavored preparation), in a sauce or sautéed, stuffed, or à la provençale, even heaped into small model fishing boats that have been patiently crafted— during stormy weather no doubt.

- **With whom:** your next crew.
- **Where:** 34, rue de Richelieu, 1st. Tel.: 42.96.06.86. Just opposite the Molière fountain.
- **When:** from noon to 2 p.m. and 7:30 to 10 p.m.; closed Saturday at noon and all day Sunday, and for one month between April and May.
- **Recommended:** mussels sautéed with salicornes (a seaweed-like vegetable), brochette of scallops, honey and nut ice cream; simple wines from the Vendée and the Loire.
- **Not recommended:** ordering two mussel dishes. Enough is enough.
- **Welcome:** hale and hearty, with rolled-up sleeves.
- **Dress:** like Walter Matthau.
- **Bottom line:** cozy, as though you're sitting in a ship's hold.
- **Cost:** 160 F.
- **Emergency alternative:** *Carr's* (p. 111).

# La Cafetière

*9 p.m.*

It's been over 20 years now and "the coffee pot" hasn't aged a bit. It's true that La Cafetière's eternally youthful owners have discovered the formula for long life: two weeks of work for one, then two weeks for the other. It's called teamwork, or "cohabitation," as the French say.

Over the years the restaurant's collection of coffee pots has grown: there are now flowered, checkered, metal, and enameled ones. And the oldtime customers have become generals, local officials, or members of the Académie Française.

This typically Parisian, cozy little group huddle together on the main floor to enjoy satisfying, regional dishes, washed down with champagne served in a carafe —the height of elegance.

- o **With whom:** a friend who needs comforting.
- o **Where:** 21 rue Mazarine, 6th. Tel.: 46.33.76.90. Opposite the Alcazar nightclub. Only the ground floor is worthy of you.
- o **When:** every day from noon to 2 p.m. and 8 to 10:30 p.m.
- o **Recommended:** eggs *en meurette* (poached in wine) or brioche with marrow, rare filet of beef à la meldoise (with a sauce made from Meaux mustard) or wild duck with celery purée; a carafe of bubbly.
- o **Welcome:** royal.
- o **Dress:** affected.
- o **Bottom line:** while gallery-hopping.
- o **Cost:** 250 F. . . . no kidding!
- o **Emergency alternative:** *Le Temps Perdu*, 54, rue de Seine, 6th. Tel.: 46.34.12.08. Literati and neighborhood gallery owners like it. Who knows why?

# La Cagouille

**9 p.m.**

La Cagouille, named after the little snails from Charentes, recently moved to new quarters on the ground floor of an antiseptic new housing development. Don't be turned off by the façade, which looks like a modern storefront: inside, the décor is as clean and bracing as a spray of sea air, with Scandinavian-style furnishings in natural wood and a glass wall divider filled with shells. Accessories are kept to a minimum; even fish knives and forks have been eliminated, although fish is the specialty.

And what fish! The catch is always fresh, personally selected by the owner every morning at the Rungis market. The day's menu is simply written on a blackboard.

The shrimp are cooked live, the salmon is grilled only on one side *(unilatérallement)* so it won't be dried out, and the red mullet is perfectly sautéed in olive oil. It's all generously washed down with the house wine, a Coteaux-du-Roannais, and an old cognac, which the bearded owner insists on serving you himself from his collection at the bar.

- **With whom:** an old salt.

- **Where:** 10–12, place Brancusi, 14th. Tel.: 43.22.09.01. Near avenue du Maine, just off rue de l'Ouest. Reserve ahead of time; there are only ten tables.

- **When:** from noon to 2 p.m. and 7:30 to 11 p.m.; closed Sunday and Monday.

- **Recommended:** you can trust the suggestions of the day. For example, pan-cooked shrimp and salmon *à l'unilatéral*, followed by a parfait of honey and pine nuts; Coteaux-du-Roannais. And a cognac, of course.

- **Welcome:** calm and kindly.

- **Dress:** anything from an old winegrower's smock to Wimbledon whites.

- **Bottom line:** perhaps the best fish bistro in Paris—certainly the friendliest.
- **Cost:** 250 F.
- **Emergency alternative:** try *La Fortune des Mers*, 55, avenue d'Italie, 13th. Tel.: 45.85.76.83. A veritable supermarket: bistro downstairs, bourgeois restaurant upstairs, and fish bar with a 39.50 F. special (which is good and fast if you have to lunch with a bore, without being insulting).

# *Chiberta* ♥

Chiberta lights up like a La Tour painting. Against a background of dark lacquer, smoked mirrors, and black screens, several splashes of color stand out: large luminous watercolors, fresh floral bouquets, and big tables that are, for a change, well spaced.

There's a certain Japanese-style elegance—restrained, vigorous, and delicate—that helps create a serene atmosphere, making this a perfect place for those important dinners on the town.

Here, nouvelle cuisine is understated: the tiny carved vegetables are not done to excess, and the menu changes so often that you can trust the suggestions of the maître d'. But based on past experience, you'll probably reorder the wonderful tartare of lobster and the granité (iced purée) of pears with chocolate and nuts. It's easy to fall into old habits at Chiberta.

- **With whom:** business partners you want to spoil; or else, why not with a romantic partner?
- **Where:** 3, rue Arsène-Houssaye, 8th. Tel.: 45.63.77.90. Between the Champs-Élysées and avenue de Friedland, close to the place de l'Étoile.
- **When:** from noon to 2 p.m. and 8 to 10:30 p.m.; closed Saturday and Sunday. Reserve in advance.
- **Recommended:** nouvelle cuisine which uses what's in season. Follow the waiter's suggestions, or take a *marbré de rouget* (filet of red mullet garnished with olives and lemon) and a pear granité; an excellent selection of burgundys.
- **Welcome:** refined but personal.
- **Dress:** sober and discreet.
- **Bottom line:** an elegant evening.
- **Cost:** 400 F.
- **Emergency alternative:** *Taillevent* (p. 63).

# Dodin Bouffant

**9 p.m.**

Here, in the most casual (pinstripes optional—a sports jacket will do) of the great Parisian restaurants, you're greeted unaffectedly with a smile. The decor is also casual—a wool fabric covering bare stone walls, and a jolly portrait of someone raising his glass.

The restaurant is worthy of the legendary gastronome for whom it's named: thin slices of foie gras in the *salade folle* ("crazy salad") top a bundle of fresh green beans, crisp carrots, and tender coquilles Saint-Jacques. The mullet, presented on a bed of sweet pepper, could inspire a still-life, and the raspberry soufflé is famous.

The prices are still reasonable, and if you know any graduate students worried about exams, you could, in good conscience, bet them a meal at Dodin Bouffant that they'll pass.

- **With whom:** presentable friends.
- **Where:** 25, rue Frédéric-Sauton, 5th. Tel.: 43.25.25.14. Down from the place Maubert. Make sure you're seated on the ground floor.
- **When:** from noon to 2:15 p.m. and 8 p.m. to 1 a.m.; closed Sunday.
- **Recommended:** the *salade folle* or marinated herring, coquilles Saint-Jacques, raspberry soufflé; the wine selection of the month.
- **Welcome:** elegant.
- **Dress:** casual, but elegant.
- **Bottom line:** a reasonably priced gastronomic evening out.
- **Cost:** 300 F.
- **Emergency alternative:** *Bofinger* (p. 167) or *Le Pacote*, 44 boulevard Saint-Germain, 5th. Tel.: 43.26.92.28. Until 11 p.m.

# Les Fusains ♥

## 9 p.m.

Let yourself be swept away to Les Fusains. Settle into this little corner house, put yourself entirely in the hands of the smiling owner who wears topsiders and a long apron, and can't resist the pleasure of adding an extra dish when you order the "menu dégustation" (the tasting menu).

And what a menu! This place is on a par with the best of them, beginning with the soft candlelight, the fresh flower bouquets, and the down-to-earth welcome.

Les Fusains is a "must" for many celebrities, but please, let them dine in peace. Don't break the spell.

- o **With whom:** real friends.
- o **Where:** 44, rue Joseph-de-Maistre, 18th. Tel.: 42.28.03.69. From place Clichy, cross the Montmartre cemetery, following it along the left-hand side.
- o **When:** from 8 p.m. to midnight; closed Sunday and Monday. Reservations recommended. From time to time, the owner takes a day off. He's entitled.
- o **Recommended:** no set menu. Choose from the handwritten list. For example: steamed scallops with hearts of lettuce and parsley, frogs' legs with oysters and crisp onion, salmon marinière, cheese, and three desserts.
- o **Welcome:** considerate.
- o **Dress:** anything goes.
- o **Bottom line:** an experience delicate as a charcoal sketch ("un fusain").
- o **Cost:** 265 F. net for the fixed menu.
- o **Emergency alternative:** *Le Clodenis*, 57, rue Caulaincourt, 18th. Tel.: 46.06.20.26. Like a salmon-colored candybox, equally hospitable and relaxing; the creation of a young Japanese chef who is perfectly at home in France. 250 F.

# Le Gourmet des Ternes

9 p.m.

The foremost gourmet of Ternes is the owner himself, who has a deep sense of professional responsibility. At daybreak, he personally selects his fresh products at Rungis, then welcomes his customers, oversees the careful cooking of the meat, keeps an eye on each table, and takes the time to see his patrons to the door with a smile.

His artichokes are never anything but fresh, his plump *piece de boeuf* (side of beef) is superb, and his peach Melba will leave you in a state of bliss.

Snobs, stars, and "creative" types all come to this simple, unpretentious place. So far they haven't spoiled it.

- **With whom:** good friends, even chic ones.
- **Where:** 87, boulevard de Courcelles, 8th. Tel.: 42.27.43.04. Next to place des Ternes.
- **When:** from noon to 2:30 p.m. and 8 to 10 p.m.; closed Saturday and Sunday.
- **Recommended:** celery rémoulade, artichoke bottoms, or *salade de boeuf, piece de boeuf*, peach Melba or baba au rhum; Chenas.
- **Welcome:** professional.
- **Dress:** relaxed.
- **Bottom line:** a reliable, honest, and friendly bistro.
- **Cost:** 150 F.
- **Emergency alternative:** *Rech*, 62, avenue des Ternes, 17th. Tel.: 45.72.28.91. Just as conscientious, offering oysters, grilled fish, its famous Camembert, and a matchless chocolate eclair. Also, *Il était une oie dans le Sud-Ouest*, a restaurant-grocery store at 8, rue Gustave-Flaubert, 17th. Tel.: 43.80.18.30. Foie gras, cassoulets, and *magrets de canard* (sliced duck filets) just like down on the farm, in a cheerful ambience.

# Chez Guyvonne

**9 p.m.**

Far from the madding crowd, Monceau Park is a quiet retreat. The people who live around it have never known it to be otherwise.

Guyvonne reflects this serenity. In an authentically rural setting, decorated with portraits and still-lifes, you can dine comfortably and become better acquainted with your business associates.

Monsieur Cros, a great and modest chef, will lend a hand—waiting on you attentively and personally preparing his awesome warm appetizers, a seafood salad, perfectly cooked fish, and a "délice d'Isabelle" which, in itself, could establish his reputation as a master pastry chef.

- **With whom:** a business associate and spouse.
- **Where:** 14, rue de Thann, 17th. Tel.: 42.27.25.43. Starting from the Rotonde of the Park Monceau, boulevard de Courcelles.
- **When:** from noon to 2 p.m. and 7:30 to 10 p.m.; closed Saturday, Sunday, and holidays.
- **Recommended:** the seafood salad, fish of the day, délice d'Isabelle.
- **Welcome:** friendly.
- **Dress:** unrestrained elegance.
- **Bottom line:** forget about the office—relax.
- **Cost:** 300 F.
- **Emergency alternative:** *Petrus*, 12, place du Maréchal-Juin, 17th. Tel.: 43.80.15.95. For perfect seafood, fine fish, and good service.

# Robuchon (formerly Jamin)  ♥

9 p.m.

All the great food critics unanimously agreed on the superiority of Jamin, which effortlessly collected prizes, stars, and toques. So the restaurant, now renamed Robuchon, doesn't have to act serious and pompous in order to attract a business-lunch crowd.

But owner Joël Robuchon seems to prefer his evening customers, who look for a little charm and folly. Robuchon's pink and marble décor is designed to flatter them.

Many women come here to exchange confidences, or they come with a male companion, knowing they'll look fetching in the soft glow of hurricane lamps and the elegant decor.

Robuchon is a brilliant innovator who has remained modest. He knows how to bring out the true flavor of a lamb roast, of a potato purée, or a crème caramel, while at the same time introducing superb new creations that consistently hit the mark.

- **With whom:** a dearly beloved.
- **Where:** 32, rue de Longchamp, 16th. Tel.: 47.27.12.27. Between avenue Kléber and Iéna; guaranteed parking. Reserve far in advance and, if possible, get a settee for two.
- **When:** from 12:30 to 2:30 p.m. and 8 to 10 p.m.; closed Saturday and Sunday.
- **Recommended:** the "menu dégustation" (a tasting menu) or, among the specialties: crayfish ravioli with cabbage, roast lamb in a salt crust, potato purée, suprême of pigeon and foie gras, crème caramel, and to top it all off, Dom Perignon.
- **Welcome:** grand.
- **Dress:** just like everyone else there—Omar Sharif and the Rothschilds.
- **Bottom line:** sheer extravagance.
- **Cost:** 700 F.
- **Emergency alternative:** *Chiberta* (p. 136).

# Lous Landes

**9 p.m.**

At Lous Landes, the essential ingredients for a fête are family, music, and heaps of food.

You're greeted by everyone's idea of the perfect grandmother: pink, plump, and dimpled, glowing with kindness and eternal youth, lovingly backed by her sturdy, friendly son.

The setting is delightfully bourgeois, right out of a Vuillard painting. Shelves are lined with jars of preserves, and the souvenirs of a lifetime are on proud display in the dining room.

Adding a dash of refinement: Mozart is sometimes played in the background, subtly underlining the delicacy of the foie gras en papillote or the fantastic prune tart.

- **With whom:** your spouse, or friendly relatives.
- **Where:** 157, avenue du Maine, 14th. Tel.: 45.43.08.04. Music two or three evenings a month. Reserve.
- **When:** from 12:30 to 2:30 p.m. and 8 to 10:30 p.m.; closed all day Sunday and Monday at noon.
- **Recommended:** papillote of foie gras, raw wild salmon, filet of duck, and prune tart; accompanied by a first-class Madiran.
- **Not recommended:** roasted oysters with saffron.
- **Welcome:** genuinely sincere.
- **Dress:** for an elegant evening out.
- **Bottom line:** for a wedding anniversary, or with a group of friends.
- **Cost:** 300 F. for four courses, music included; lunch menu at 220 F.
- **Emergency alternative:** *Le Duc*, 243 boulevard Raspail, 14th. Tel.: 43.20.96.30.

# La Maison Blanche  ♥

**9 p.m.**

Porte de Versailles
To be seen

Only one dazzling restaurant could draw the glitterati of Paris all the way out past the Porte de Versailles. But its sudden and unexpected success hasn't gone to the head of this "White House": neither the folks from TV station Canal Plus nor the Paris movers and shakers and their hangers-on can lure José Lampreia out of his kitchen.

Passionate about his creations, he has devoted himself to renewing regional dishes with consummate mastery. The *gâteau landais* is studded with foie gras, the *brandade* (usually made with cod) made with haddock, and cabbage stuffed with oysters.

The decor, brightened by copious bouquets of white tulips, is both sober and fresh, with a touch of humor in the bathrooms, where multiple mirrors reflect your image to infinity.

- **With whom:** a woman in white.
- **Where:** 82, boulevard Lefèbvre, 15th. Tel.: 48.28.38.83. Past the Palais des Expositions, on the same side.
- **When:** Every day except Sunday, Monday, and Saturday at noon.
- **Recommended:** everything, and especially the cabbage stuffed with oysters, lotte with eggplant and red peppers, *fondant* with chocolate, rum, and raisins. And a vintage "Brut Imperial" for the show.
- **Welcome:** a delicious hostess and a stylish maître d'.
- **Dress:** *haute couture* at the first seating, designer ready-to-wear clothes at the second.
- **Bottom line:** relaxed gastronomy.
- **Cost:** 250 F.; lunch menu at 180 F.
- **Emergency alternative:** Another rising star, on the other side of town: *Apicus*, 122, avenue de Villiers, 17th. Tel.: 43.80.19.66. An equally sparkling cuisine, but decidedly more expensive, with over-refined service, a lackluster clientele, and a touch of pretension.

DINNERS FOR SPECIAL OCCASIONS   143

# Au Quai des Ormes ♥

**9 p.m.**

♈ ♈

You'll find the elm trees ("les ormes") in a peaceful Piedmontaise landscape painted in Italian fresco style on the walls of the dining room. Green carpeting, a rose trellis, and floral fabrics further foster the illusion of an indoor garden. And the friendly smile of the hostess is enough to make you forget the rigors of your day in Paris.

In this serene setting, a light cuisine is all the more welcome. The fixed menu called *"au bonheur des dames"* has only 900 calories, but is a far cry from dismal diet fare: it includes marinated salmon, veal kidney fricassée with tarragon, and nougat ice cream with cherries.

Big eaters will prefer a super-sensual salad of sautéed sweetbreads with tarragon, a tender saddle of young rabbit with wild mushrooms, and the special house dessert: a marvelous *chaud-froid* of pears (warm) with pistachio ice cream (cold).

- **With whom:** a weight-conscious dancer.
- **Where:** 72, quai de l'Hôtel-de-Ville, 4th. Tel.: 42.74.72.22. Between Pont Louis-Philippe and the Hôtel de Ville (City Hall). Parking nearby at Pont Marie. Private dining rooms and a terrace overlooking the Seine.
- **When:** from 12:30 to 2:30 p.m. and 8 to 10:30 p.m.; closed Saturday and Sunday.
- **Recommended:** the diet menu or, à la carte, the veal kidney and the *chaud-froid* of pears and pistachio; Cahors '82 Domaine de Ceret Montpezat, or reasonably priced bordeaux.
- **Welcome:** charming.
- **Dress:** Florentine.
- **Bottom line:** have dinner and unwind.
- **Cost:** 300 F.
- **Emergency alternative:** *Dodin Bouffant* (p. 137).

# Country-Style Dinners

*Le Chalet des Îles. Bois de Boulogne.* If you can't make up your mind between the pretentiousness of la Grande Cascade and the crowds at l'Auberge du Bonheur, and if the Pré Catelan seems too expensive, try le Chalet des Îles—the kind of place that caters weddings and banquets. Go if only for the pleasure of getting out of Paris and taking a lovers' walk on the island after dinner. The fixed menu is 161 F. Open every day until 9:30 p.m. Boat landing on the Porte de la Muette side of the Bois. Tel.: 42.88.04.69. ♟

*Le Relais du Bois. Bois de Boulogne.* The setting—a clearing at the end of the woods—is lovely, but the grilled dishes are only so-so. Kids appreciate the amusement park. Figure 120 F. From noon to 2:30 p.m. and 7 to 10 p.m.; closed Sunday evening. Tel.: 42.88. 08.43. ♟

*Restaurant du Plateau de Gravelle. Bois de Vincennes.* Devotees of the Vincennes racetrack and suburban gourmands appreciate the simple and hearty cooking at this Napoleon III hunting pavilion. A very nice garden, somewhat Japanese. Figure 200 F., or 100 F. in the annex. Open every day until 11 p.m. Tel.: 43.68.00.13. ♟ ♟

*Le Totem. Palais de Chaillot.* Wave to the Eiffel Tower from behind a monumental stone bison—a relic from the Universal Exposition—standing on the terrace of the Musée de l'Homme. The buffet is a good value at 61.50 F., as is the fixed menu at 200 F. But beware of anything more exotic than the crudités at the buffet. Expect lackadaisical service. Open from noon to 3 p.m. and 7:30 to 10:30 p.m.; closed Tuesday. 1, place du Trocadéro, 16th. Tel.: 47.27.74.11. ♟

# On the Difficulty of Being
# Au Courant

"Rad" one day, "bad" the next, "hot" or "hip" another evening—the vocabulary is as faddish as the fashions. How can anyone keep up?

Reading *City, Passion, Actuel,* and *Libération* isn't enough. You have to be the first to know about the latest sensation at Pacific Palisade's, the opening of a new lunch spot by a top model, or the rediscovery of *Le Train Bleu.*

The rewards of your success? You will feel perfectly at ease among gorgeous waitresses, haughtily elegant waiters, old-fashioned ceiling fans, and black-and-white blow-ups of Marilyn Monroe. And in the flurry of models, advertising execs, and sundry actors, you'll be able to spot the athlete who is getting out of shape and the star embroiled in a steamy scandal.

In addition to all this, don't expect to dine well. The fresh pasta will arrive cold, the carpaccio will be swimming in oil, and the tartare will have more mayonnaise than seasoning.

Here, for your edification, are the new places you simply can't ignore:

*Café de la Jatte:* 67, boulevard de Levallois, Neuilly. Tel.: 47.45.04.20. A wonderful terrace and an impressive loft located in a former stable. The current fauna (local admen) is rather flashy and the cuisine just borders on being acceptable. Cost: 200 F. Closed Saturday at noon.

*Café Mexico:* 1, place de Mexico, 16th. Tel.: 47.27.96.98. All the elements of Parisian life can be found here: men about town, stunning women, insipid but light cuisine, and art deco tables for a retro touch. Overall, a sense of déjà vu. Cost: 180 F.

**Bermuda Onion:** 16, rue de Linois, 15th. Tel.: 45.75.11.11. The most dazzling of all these places, with a decor out of *Diva*, plastic swimmers dangling from the ceiling, flirtatious waitresses, and a splendid terrace. The dishes still arrive cold and the wait is intolerable. Cost: 230 F.

# Café Max

Max is a gamesman. Not content just inventing board games, he likes to challenge his customers to the point of exasperation. By turns, he's despicable, charming, and insolent; he'll throw out anyone he doesn't like, and kiss those he does; he'll ask you to set your table yourself, and he'll enjoy your impertinent ripostes.

Apparently, cooking fascinates him less than hunting and fishing: trophies from these last two activities cover the walls. But what he likes to cook, he cooks well: a "famous salad," a huge country-style buffet, sausages with choucroute, and delicate slices of braised ham.

Don't ask him for a raspberry charlotte. He offers only one dessert, usually a warm tart—take it or leave it. You'll be glad you took it.

- **With whom:** friends who can talk back.
- **Where:** 7, avenue de la Motte-Picquet, 7th. Tel.: 47.05.57.66. Near les Invalides.
- **When:** from noon to 2 p.m. and 8 p.m. to midnight; closed Sunday.
- **Recommended:** the famous salad, the braised ham, the sausage-choucroute, the tart of the day; Bergerac wine.
- **Not recommended:** the cassoulet.
- **Welcome:** always provoking; but really warm, underneath it all.
- **Dress:** as long as Max likes what she's wearing. . . .
- **Bottom line:** to have a good time, with good friends.
- **Cost:** 80 F.
- **Emergency alternative:** just opposite, *L'Auberge Bressane*, 16, avenue de la Motte-Picquet, 7th. Tel.: 47.05.98.37.

# *Cinnamon* ♥

## *10 p.m.*

Cinnamon is a slave to fashion. The ceiling fan is there—utterly useless—as well as the ubiquitous posters of Man Ray and Andy Warhol, and the black-and-white photos of Marilyn, Marlene, and other deathless beauties. The staff can only be described as good-looking, fast-talking, and totally blasé, and the model who heads them up draws in the denizens of Castel's, the chic club around the corner.

But this place is far from shabby. Soft lighting and well-spaced tables encourage you to linger. And the cuisine, in particular, is top quality: fresh artichoke hearts, excellent vinaigrette sauces, and well-seasoned tartares.

Maybe fashion's actually becoming food-conscious?

- **With whom:** a gourmet model.
- **Where:** 30, rue Saint-Sulpice, 6th Tel · 43.26.53.33. Across from the Saint-Sulpice church.
- **When:** from noon to 3 p.m. and 7:30 to 11:30 p.m.; closed Sunday. Just as nice at noon, with a different clientele (stray senators and publishers).
- **Recommended:** artichoke hearts, seafood pot-au-feu, marquise au chocolat (mousse-like chocolate cake).
- **Welcome:** hip.
- **Dress:** fashionable.
- **Bottom line:** to be seen.
- **Cost:** 200 F.; a fixed menu at 139 F.
- **Emergency alternative:** back down to earth at *Petit Saint-Benoît*, 4, rue Saint-Benoît, 6th. Tel.: 42.60.27.92. Open from noon to 2 p.m. and 7 to 10 p.m.; closed Saturday and Sunday. 80 F. maximum, and you'll be coddled by the waitresses.

# Da Graziano

The show does still go on in Montmartre. Inside, the Italianesque décor depicts many a comedy scene, while outside, the atmosphere is carnival-like.

Cut off from the street noise by lush foliage, protected by a canopied dais, enjoy a lovers' tête-à-tête on this Venetian-inspired terrace.

Theater people, in their element, like the traditional, high-quality cuisine: tortellini à la crème, spaghetti à la vongole (clams), saltimbocca, and real Mediterranean bread, baked in the restaurant's own oven. A fine fruit mousse, light as whipped cream, tops it all off.

- **With whom:** someone who misses the romance of Venice.
- **Where:** 83, rue Lepic, 18th. Tel.: 46.06.84.77. Located at the Moulin de la Galette—which every tourist knows.
- **When:** from noon to 2:30 p.m. and 8 p.m. to 12:30 a.m.
- **Recommended:** dish of Italian charcuterie (cold cuts), tortellini à la crème, spaghetti à la vongole, saltimbocca or filet à la pizzaiola, and fruit mousse.
- **Not recommended:** carpaccio, turbot au gratin.
- **Welcome:** charming.
- **Dress:** if you've got it, flaunt it.
- **Bottom line:** like a summer meal outdoors.
- **Cost:** 250 F.
- **Emergency alternative:** *Au Petit Robert*, 10, rue Cauchois, 18th. Tel.: 46.06.04.46.

# Dave

**10 p.m.**

Winning people over without even trying—that seems to be Dave's secret. He's a big, mad Chinese guy, a remarkable host, and a despotic ruler of the place. He only accepts customers he likes; he announces his dishes in a loud voice (no written menu exists), and he constantly flits from table to table.

So why does he remain so popular with such people as filmmakers Lelouch and Godard? Why does Diana Ross come here to refuel herself after giving a concert? Why does fashion designer Jean-Paul Gaultier—and his cohorts—patronize this fearful fellow's place?

Partly because of the family-style Sino-Vietnamese cuisine, which really isn't authentic. Even more because of the host's one-man show. And most of all—at least for the celebrities—because for once they can forget the spotlights and posturing and simply be left alone.

- o **With whom:** a star, if possible.
- o **Where:** 39, rue Saint-Roch, 1st. Tel.: 42.61.49.48. Between the church and avenue de l'Opéra.
- o **When:** from noon to 2:30 p.m. and 8 to 11 p.m.; closed all day Saturday and Sunday at noon.
- o **Recommended:** you haven't any choice: the master dictates the day's menu. The spring rolls are famous; the chicken with lemon sauce and fresh fruit are recommended.
- o **Welcome:** what a show!
- o **Dress:** high fashion or young designer.
- o **Bottom line:** being there.
- o **Cost:** 150 F.
- o **Emergency alternative:** *Elmo Coppi*, 9, rue d'Argenteuil, 1st. Tel.: 42.60.56.22. Closed Saturday and Sunday. An unpretentious but attractive *trattoria*, featuring excellent food in a cozy Commedia del'Arte setting.

# *Janou*

## 10 p.m.

Janou still doesn't understand how it suddenly became chic. Its décor, similar to that of a horsemeat butcher, hasn't changed one iota, and the big circular counter leaves very little space for the bistro-style booths.

But the waiters are up-to-date: cool and supercilious, black, white, gay, and straight, with long hair or shaved heads. In summer the terrace, set back from the street, is one of the best spots in all of Paris. And last but not least, the traditional bourgeois cuisine has the merit of being perfectly simple—sometimes too much so, like the scorched sweet potatoes.

- **With whom:** someone who feels out of it.
- **Where:** 2, rue Roger-Verlomme, 3rd. Tel.: 42.72.28.41. Behind the place des Vosges, at the corner of rue des Tournelles. Well-protected terrace.
- **When:** Until 10:30 p.m.; closed Saturday and Sunday.
- **Recommended:** foie gras, confit of duck, chocolate cake or fruit soup with mint.
- **Not recommended:** any of the steaks, or the bland curry.
- **Welcome:** both bohemian and post-modern.
- **Dress:** country style.
- **Bottom line:** hip, with a retro tendency.
- **Cost:** 150 F.
- **Emergency alterantive:** *Ma Bourgogne,* 19, place des Vosges, 4th. Tel.: 42.78.44.64. Naturally rustic, and a pleasant terrace in the summer.

# *Marshal's*

The décor—hidden behind drawn Venetian blinds—
might have been created by David Hockney. It's a
successful interpretation of minimalist California modern: beige and sand tones highlighted by a few ethereal
paintings, some sturdy banana trees, and an Indian
carved in red sequoia.

The person responsible for this production is indeed
from Hollywood. A former executive at ABC television,
he watches over every detail, including his waiters, who
are spiffily dressed in the casual, elegant style you see in
yacht clubs. They tirelessly translate the menu—which
is unabashedly American—to the French customers.

You can trust them. Fresh strawberries go into the
daiquiries, and even the potato chips are homemade.
No regional specialty is overlooked, not even soft-shell
crabs: the French are amazed to discover you eat the
shell!

- **With whom:** a seasoned producer.
- **Where:** 63, avenue Franklin-Roosevelt, 8th. Tel.:
  45.63.21.22. Near Métro Saint-Philippe-de-Roule.
- **When:** every day from noon to 2:30 p.m. and 8 p.m.
  to midnight, and brunch on Sunday.
- **Recommended:** strawberry daiquiri as an apéritif,
  Caesar salad, soft-shell crabs, apple pie à la mode or
  pecan pie. And why not wash it down with a Pine
  Ridge Cabernet?
- **Not recommended:** be careful—you might land
  there on an off day.
- **Welcome:** very Yuppy.
- **Dress:** a tie, please.
- **Bottom line:** authentic California chic.
- **Cost:** 240 F.: more if you order California wines.
- **Emergency alternative:** *Le Bœuf sur le Toit*, just
  opposite (p. 166).

# *Natacha* ♥

Natacha is like a warm beach. You dine here surrounded by a photographic harem of nudes from the '30s, among palm trees and souvenirs of the Colonial Exposition. The walls look like baked clay, and you can imagine langorous Fatimas performing a belly-dance.

Fortunately, the management refuses to get caught in the exotic trap—couscous and so on—and prefers to serve light food adapted to the fashion of the times, such as carpaccio and tomato-mozzarella.

Natacha is perhaps the last restaurant in Montparnasse that still attracts photographers, actors, and models. It has succeeded, after a brief eclipse, to keep on going—although success seems to have gone to the heads of the snooty waiters.

- **With whom:** a model, if possible.
- **Where:** 17 bis, rue Campagne-Première, 14th. Tel.: 43.20.79.27. Off boulevard Montparnasse, between La Closerie and La Coupole.
- **When:** Until 1 a.m.; closed Sunday.
- **Recommended:** carpaccio or tomato-mozzarella, curry, or calf's liver, floating island (meringue floating in custard sauce).
- **Welcome:** intellectual.
- **Dress:** trendy.
- **Bottom line:** quietly exotic.
- **Cost:** 160 F.
- **Emergency alternative:** *La Coupole* (p. 170).

# *Olsson's*

The sudden appearance of windows swathed in blue and yellow—the colors of Sweden—on the aristocratic rue Pierre-Charron signaled Olsson's move from the run-down Beaubourg area to a space near the Champs-Élysées. The new place has high ceilings, gray striped wallpaper, and two grand fireplaces, but the same beautiful blondes are still here to wait on you, with their delightfully accented French. The models—from *Mademoiselle* and elsewhere—have followed, joined by the after-cinema crowd. The Swedish menu with French subtitles is still the same too, with its spicy marinades and wonderful desserts; by serving small portions Olsson's makes a real effort to keep the cuisine light.

Coming up in the world hasn't caused Olsson's to lose its main attraction: freshness.

- **With whom:** a misty blonde.

- **Where:** 62, rue Pierre-Charron, 8th. Tel.: 45.61.49.11. Between the American Legion and the Champs-Élysées, one flight up. You'll see the blue and yellow curtains.

- **When:** every day from noon to midnight.

- **Recommended:** marinated salmon or Olsson's salad, brochette with beans or quail with grapes, the famous chocolate-lemon cake; acquavit. Excellent bread.

- **Not recommended:** very salty marinated herring, and the Karl Gustav platter (which takes some getting used to).

- **Welcome:** utterly charming.

- **Dress:** leather or linen.

- **Bottom line:** nice after a movie.

- **Cost:** 200 F.

○ **Emergency alternative:** *La Fermette Marbeuf*, 5, rue Marbeuf, 8th. Tel.: 47.20.63.53. 250 F. Service until 11:30 p.m. Worth it, if only to see the marvelous turn-of-the century garden room, with its original stained glass.

# *Le Pastel* ♥

## 10 p.m.

An ideal setting for a bash celebrating the première of a grade-B movie—or maybe B+. The owner—a dead ringer for the scruffy French singer, Serge Gainsbourg—wears faded jeans and a bow tie, and personally welcomes his peers: producers he thinks are important, starlets he likes to pinch, and the usual opening-night crowd.

The cuisine, which leans toward the scrambled-eggs-and-leeks school of down-to-earth cooking, is self-consciously simple. But who cares about that, as long as everyone is having a good time.

The pianist, who has been doggedly pounding out Simon and Garfunkel songs to an indifferent audience, is delighted when some amateur singers chime in. Pretty soon, the more adventuresome scrawl their name, telephone number, or their thought for the day on the pastel walls. When the walls are scrubbed down, they start over. You get used to it.

- **With whom:** someone who's mad about Rambo.
- **Where:** 60, rue Rambuteau, 3rd. Tel.: 42.77.08.27. Between boulevard Sébastopol and the Pompidou Center, next to rue Quincampoix.
- **When:** from noon to 3 p.m. and 8:30 p.m. to 12:30 a.m.; closed Sunday at noon and Monday evening. Come after 11 p.m. for the show-biz atmosphere.
- **Recommended:** scrambled eggs with salmon, filet of sole with salmon.
- **Not recommended:** filet of duck with three fruits, the pies.
- **Welcome:** blasé.
- **Dress:** relaxed.
- **Bottom line:** to show off your latest starlet.
- **Cost:** 200 F.
- **Emergency alternative:** *Pacific Palisade's*, the original "in" place, 51, rue Quincampoix, 4th. Tel.: 42.74.01.17.

# Le Petit Poucet ♥

## 10 p.m.

Île de la Jatte
Country tavern

When will country taverns (*guinguettes*) make a comeback? Nostalgic fans of Jean Renoir films would like to revive them, along with the popular dance halls that flourished on the Île de la Jatte.

It's easy for such sentimentalists to console themselves at Le Petit Poucet, sitting on the terrace during a heat wave, counting the houseboats, or simply commenting on the cars people drive up in.

A bit snobbish, they never fail to recognize such and such a star, advertising tycoons, or a racecar driver. Many are inveterate womanizers, who hungrily eye their dates—or the mini-clad waitresses who may become their dates one day. Feigning simplicity, they relish the fresh cuisine (green beans, carpaccio) and adore the luscious, chilled chocolate cake, which deserves a special mention.

- **With whom:** a Grand Prix racing circuit beauty.
- **Where:** 1, boulevard de Levallois. Tel.: 47.38.61.85. On the Île de la Jatte, immortalized by artists; on the right-hand side coming from Neuilly.
- **When:** from noon to 2:30 p.m. and 8 to 11 p.m.; closed Saturday and Sunday at noon (also closed in the winter).
- **Recommended:** carpaccio, tartare, chocolate cake (which, alas, is rarely on the menu anymore).
- **Welcome:** very seductive.
- **Dress:** dandified.
- **Bottom line:** the *guinguette* Jet Set.
- **Cost:** 180 F.
- **Emergency alternative:** *La Guinguette de Neuilly*, right next door at 12, boulevard de Levallois. Tel.: 46.24.26.04. 160 F. And *Les Pieds dans l'Eau*, 39, boulevard du Parc; a terrace on the banks of the Seine, with passable cuisine. Tel.: 47.47.64.07. 240 F.

# *Le Potager des Halles* ♥

## 10 p.m.

Stretch out on the terrace among the plunging décolletés and the daringly slit skirts; saunter into the ground-floor dining room, decorated with watery frescoes; admire the pirouettes of the feline waitresses and their muscular colleagues; or else join the discreet, sedate clientele on the upper floor.

Le Potager des Halles has never been disappointing, and even the most blasé night owls make sure to reserve a table in advance, in order to enjoy a "salade minceur" (a low-calorie salad) half-hidden under a *crottin de Chavignol* cheese, calves' liver garnished with broccoli (the ultimate culinary chic), and airy desserts like mousses and sorbets.

- **With whom:** a fashion plate.
- **Where:** 15, rue des Cygnes, 1st. Tel.: 42.96.83.30. At the entrance to the car tunnel, on the boulevard de Sébastopol side. Reserve in advance and arrive on time.
- **When:** from noon to 1 a.m.; closed Sunday.
- **Recommended:** warm *crottin de Chavignol*, chocolate *fondat*.
- **Welcome:** more to be seen than served.
- **Dress:** a Jean-Paul Gaultier outfit.
- **Bottom line:** to show off your companion.
- **Cost:** 180 F.
- **Emergency alternative:** *Chez Vong*, 10 rue de la Grande-Truanderie, 1st. Tel.: 42.96.29.89. Straight out of Charlie Chan: winding corridors, half-drawn blinds, backrooms lit with candles . . . guaranteed charm, with gastronomy to match, for 250 F.

# Le Pupillin

If you're off on a new romantic adventure, you can start it here, at this Fellini-esque watering hole.

It's updated Fellini, to be sure, with well-dressed Yuppies propped against the wine bar, nibbling on a light snack and sipping a good wine. Or they're up-stairs, among the sensual blow-ups of luscious grapes and the posters of famous films.

Though located in a marginal neighborhood, this is an impeccable place, where you can overhear your neighbors' mutterings about Life and Love, eye the charming waitresses, and relish the light (but not nou-velle) cuisine: spinach salad with *fourme d'Ambert* cheese, raw marinated fish, and the "After Eight"—a genoise cake with minty chocolate.

- **With whom:** creative types.
- **Where:** 19, rue Notre-Dame-de-Lorette, 9th. Tel.: 42.85.46.06. Go to place Saint Georges and then down rue Notre-Dame-de-Lorette.
- **When:** every evening, except Sunday, until 1:30 a.m.
- **Recommended:** raw spinach salad with *fourme d'Ambert* cheese, nougat ice cream with fruit sauce, or the "After Eight."
- **Welcome:** delightful.
- **Dress:** meticulous.
- **Bottom line:** to grasp the meaning of life . . . or at least gab about it.
- **Cost:** 120 F.
- **Emergency alterantive:** *Haynes* (p. 114).

# Le XVI^e

The 16th arrondissement is the home of Paris's affluent youth, nicknamed Nappies (for Neuilly, Auteuil, and Passy—the three upscale neighborhoods). Their style isn't Hermès scarf/pearl necklace, but rather, Porsche/Ray-Ban.

The recently renovated Le XVI is their bistro. It exudes an air of Saint-Tropez, with the bustle and improvisation of a lazy summer evening. Mirrors reflect the young Narcissi, and the endless conversations grind on about Art and the best way to get a tan.

"Le easy way of eating" is the big thing here. Wolfing down fresh pasta in the swanky 16th is the thing to do.

- **With whom:** show-off teeny-boppers.
- **Where:** 18, rue des Belles-Feuilles, 16th. Tel.: 47.04.56.33. Next to Janson-de-Sailly, the city's chic-est high school.
- **When:** from noon to 2:30 p.m. and 8 to 10:45 p.m.; closed Sunday.
- **Recommended:** fettuccine with tomato and basil, tartare, chocolate *fondant.*
- **Not recommended:** chicken brochettes.
- **Welcome:** distracted; they're still upset over the renovation.
- **Dress:** Beach Boy.
- **Bottom line:** meet here before going dancing at Castel's.
- **Cost:** 140 F.
- **Emergency alternative:** *Café Mexico* (p. 146), in the same vein, or for something more authentic, *Le Restaurant des Chauffeurs*, 8, chaussée de la Muette, 16th. Tel.: 42.88.50.05. Where the Countess of Paris rubs elbows with taxi drivers. It's true—the fixed menu costs only 44 F.

# Le Volant

Race car drivers lead fast lives—on and off the circuit. Le Volant, a friendly bistro run by a former champion, gives these guys an excuse to celebrate their accomplishments and show off their gorgeous girlfriends. The fast lane is a charmed circle.

Look at the walls for a pictorial history of the racing exploits of the owner, Georges Houel, during the '50s: races in Corsica, over the Alps, and so on.

Still ready to take off for Le Mans or the Paris–Dakar, this septuagenarian is also a former butcher, so he's scrupulously careful about the meat he serves. And he's warm and hospitable.

- **With whom:** a race car fan.
- **Where:** 13, rue Béatrice-Dussane, 15th. Tel.: 45.75.27.67. From the elevated Métro station, down rue de Lourmel, second street on the left.
- **When:** from noon to 3 p.m. and 8 to 11 p.m.; closed Saturday at noon and all day Sunday.
- **Recommended:** roquefort salad, "effet de sole" with shallots (a play on words, understood only by the drivers: it's actually a steak), prunes with wine.
- **Welcome:** chummy.
- **Dress:** leather, of course.
- **Bottom line:** for autograph hunters or gawkers.
- **Cost:** 75 F. for the fixed menu, 140 F. à la carte.
- **Emergency alternative:** *Le Commerce*, 51 rue du Commerce, 15th. Tel.: 45.75.03.27. From 11:45 a.m. to 2:45 p.m. and 6:30 to 9:45 p.m. Unbelievably honky-tonk and small-town on both floors, with generous waitresses, and a fixed menu for about 50 F. At this price, don't expect quality too.

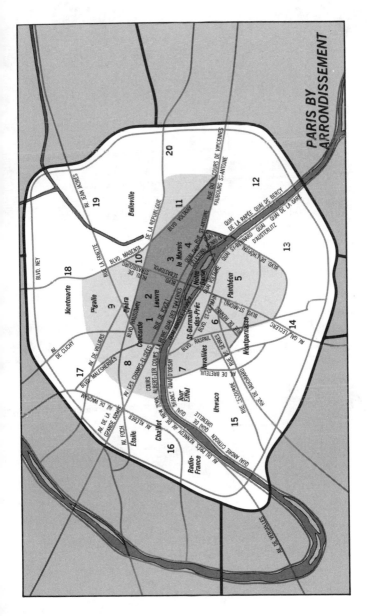

PARIS BY
ARRONDISSEMENT

PARIS ARRONDISSEMENTS 163

**Midnight**

*Late Supper*
*Late Bars*
*First-stop Nightclubs*

# Le Bœuf sur le Toit

## Midnight

Champs-Élysées
F. Scott Fitzgerald

Le Bœuf sur le Toit is the name of a ballet of the '20s, based on a text by Jean Cocteau, with music by Darius Milhaud and choreography by Massine. It was revived 60 years later under the jaundiced eye of Picabia, falling into a time warp that makes it seem more surrealistic than ever.

Flappers no longer do the Charleston here, but elegant women still sway to the tempo thumped out by the black piano player.

And the beat goes on. Those who attended the opening of this place in 1921 return now with young women of the '80s. Jean-Paul Belmondo and other stars keep the place humming, under the square art deco cupola.

- **With whom:** a Coco-girl (Coco Chanel, that is).
- **Where:** 34, rue du Colisée, 8th. Tel.: 43.59.83.80. Between avenue Franklin-Roosevelt and faubourg Saint-Honoré. Insist on a table in the main room, not upstairs.
- **When:** Every day from noon to 3 p.m. and 7 p.m. to 2 a.m.
- **Recommended:** the seafood platter (superb, for two people), lotte with green pepper, delicate apple tart.
- **Not recommended:** the salade riche, with foie gras—too much of a good thing.
- **Welcome:** as at a brasserie—curt but kind.
- **Dress:** with care: you have to walk through a long room, under the scrutiny of an elite audience.
- **Bottom line:** to be seen in the latest Parisian setting.
- **Cost:** 230 F.
- **Emergency alternative:** the first Bœuf sur le Toit is still around. First class, with its 19th-century ceramics, its maîtres d' dressed up like pashas. Top quality seafood, but frankly, too expensive. Figure more than 300 F. (after all, you're right across from the Ritz). Goumard, 17, rue Duphot, 1st. Tel.: 42.60.36.07.

# Bofinger

## Midnight

You could have been coming to Bofinger since 1864 but never thought about going upstairs. And why should you have, when you enjoyed eating under the glass ceiling in the big brasserie-style dining room, among the carved swans and flowers, and liked stealing downstairs to admire the dolphin-decorated rest rooms and the mosaic of a vampish, allegorical Science (who looks more like an homage to Gastronomy than to knowledge).

But the more sober upstairs also deserves your attention: small salons are decorated with art deco marquetry, and the Alsatian room is hung with museum-quality paintings by Hansi.

Bofinger does best with its classic dishes (foie gras with choucroute) and its desserts, which will satisfy even an Alsatian appetite. It's one of those rare brasseries where you still feel you're getting a proper welcome.

- **With whom:** a tableful of good friends.
- **Where:** 5-7, rue de la Bastille, 4th. Tel.: 42.72.87.82. Between the Bastille and rue de la Tournelle.
- **When:** every day from noon to 3 p.m. and 7:30 p.m. to 1 a.m.
- **Recommended:** foie gras, peasant choucroute or coquilles Saint-Jacques; Tokay.
- **Not recommended:** filet of duck, tartare.
- **Welcome:** by an entire team.
- **Dress:** well turned-out.
- **Bottom line:** the best brasserie in Paris.
- **Cost:** 160 F.
- **Emergency alternative:** *Jenny* (p. 171).

# La Brasserie de l'Île Saint-Louis

## *Midnight*

Île Saint-Louis
Polyglot

Yvon has been working here for 24 years, and has a statue of himself at Paris's Modern Art Museum. Impeccable, wrapped in his black vest and long white apron, he calls out to his customers in a raucous voice, with a perfect mixture of teasing, joking, and smiling.

People from the island or just passing through adore this place, and automatically claim it as "their" brasserie. It's the real Alsace, with a well-worn bar built on barrels, light fixtures attached to buckets, grape-picking baskets in the corners, and a stork on the counter.

And what's more, every tasty dish is tagged with a pun. For the British, "to beer or not to beer"; for the Americans, "cassious clay"; and so on for the Germans and the rest. For the French, there's always the good humor of the waiters.

- **With whom:** other foreigners.
- **Where:** 55, quai de Bourbon, 4th. Tel.: 43.54.02.59. At the tip of the island, opposite Notre-Dame.
- **When:** from noon to 1:30 a.m.; closed Wednesday and Thursday until 6 p.m.
- **Recommended:** *mâche* (lamb's lettuce) and beet salad, calves' liver or choucroute, crème caramel or Melba, and draft beer, naturally.
- **Not recommended:** curly endive salad with bacon.
- **Welcome:** typical oldtime waiters.
- **Dress:** "Île Saint-Louis" flannel.
- **Bottom line:** for Sunday supper, after a day in the country.
- **Cost:** 120 F.

- **Emergency alternative:** *l'Orangerie*, 28, rue Saint-Louis-en-l'Île, 4th. Tel.: 46.33.93.98. From 8:30 p.m. to midnight (two sittings). Reserve in advance. Recommended for the 17th-century setting, the sumptuous flower arrangements, the seriousness of the maître d' who recites the menu to you, the green bean salad with foic gras, and the tourists from the Middle West. 270 F.

# La Coupole   ♥

## Midnight

Every true Parisian has gone, goes, or will go to La
Coupole. A café, a bar, a restaurant, a dance hall—this
vast, noisy brasserie is steeped in tradition. Even its
square pillars are sacrosanct: they've been painted by
practically every artist—well known, and little known
—of the Paris School.

Fashionably anti-fashion, La Coupole is highly theatrical. Couples automatically sit side-by-side on the
banquettes so they can take in the scene.

While enjoying dishes that are kept deliberately simple, you'll run into folks from the provinces who have
had their fill of Parisian life, tourists who have dropped
in for a quick look, elderly ladies, self-styled artists,
inveterate night-prowlers, deputies coming from a late
session of the National Assembly, and, always, very
pretty women.

Some things never change.

- **With whom:** an eccentric Parisian, or a dowdy
  provincial.
- **Where:** 102, boulevard du Montparnasse, 14th.
  Tel.: 43.20.14.20. Palatial and unmistakable on the
  boulevard.
- **When:** every day from noon to 2 a.m.
- **Recommended:** oysters, tartare or lamb curry,
  profiteroles.
- **Not recommended:** the choucroute.
- **Welcome:** efficient, professional.
- **Dress:** so you'll be noticed.
- **Bottom line:** to be seen after the theater.
- **Cost:** 150 F.
- **Emergency alternative:** *Le Dôme*, the eternal chal-
  lenger, 108, boulevard du Montparnesse, 14th. Tel.:
  43.35.25.91.

# Jenny

## Midnight

République
Breughelian

♈ ♈ ♈

The locals have never lost confidence in Jenny, who continues to nourish them as heartily as she did in the days when Maurice Chevalier dropped by often.

But Jenny doesn't seem to have much confidence in the locals, or at least in local products. All the charcuterie (cold cuts) are German—Leberwurst (liver sausage) or Presskopf (head cheese)—and the enormous portions of choucroute are from Alsace.

The waitresses aren't disguised as peasant girls—they really are peasant girls from Alsace. Painted landscapes of grape harvesting also evoke that region, and the heavy light fixtures will delight admirers of Gallé, the Alsace-Lorraine glassmaker.

- o **With whom:** heavy eaters.
- o **Where:** 39, boulevard du Temple, 3rd. Tel.: 42.74.75.75. At the beginning of the boulevard, on place de la République.
- o **When:** every day from 11:30 a.m. to 1 a.m. Don't go on Saturday night or Sunday at noon—it's too crowded.
- o **Recommended:** apart from the choucroute, take nothing for granted. Try the peasant choucroute or Jenny's Special, then the Vosgienne meringue; Tokay 77.
- o **Welcome:** gruff but straightforward.
- o **Dress:** elbow patches.
- o **Bottom line:** for a real choucroute.
- o **Cost:** 140 F.
- o **Emergency alternative:** *Bofinger* (p. 167).

# Le Kokolion

*Midnight*

With courage and cunning, Le Kokolion has been able to protect itself against invading tourists and nostalgia buffs (and there are hordes of both in Montmarte) thanks to its strange name (half-cock, half-lion), its uninviting grillwork, and a sealed double door.

So, arriving after the theater, you'll have to knock hard to get into this scenic place where the mistress of the house is a featured player.

While your neighbors are loudly lamenting "the depressing world of the artist," you'll be digging into some solid country food—cheese vacherin (like a raclette) and the "Super Kokolian" (pound cake smothered in crème fraîche and jam)—which will put you in the mood to sit back and watch the show around you. The fourth act, so to speak.

- **With whom:** a rising young star.
- **Where:** 62, rue d'Orsel, 18th. Tel.: 42.58.24.41. In front of the Atelier Theater, going toward rue des Abbesses.
- **When:** from 8 p.m. to 1 a.m.; closed Sunday.
- **Dress:** for evening, for town, or for the stage.
- **Welcome:** impeccable.
- **Recommended:** cheese vacherin, Super Kokolion.
- **Not recommended:** ratato (chocolate fondant).
- **Bottom line:** a show after the show.
- **Cost:** 160 F.
- **Emergency alternative:** *La Pomponnette*, 42, rue Lepic, 18th. Tel.: 46.06.08.36. A part of Montmartre history, but only serves until 9:30 p.m. After that, go to *Wepler* (p. 178).

# Lipp

*Midnight*

This is where politicians publicly bury the hatchet, where publishers display promising young writers, and where TV-conscious celebrities display themselves. Formerly, before the longtime director Roger Cazes passed away, you had to be accompanied by a leading legislator, a literary lion, or a theater idol in order to be seated at the Holy of Holies—the best banquette in the front room. Mere mortals were sent off to "Siberia"—the dining room on the first floor.

But since Cazes' death in the spring of 1987, Lipp has undergone a small revolution. Managed now by a woman, the restaurant stays open every day of the week, closes for only four weeks a year instead of nine, and accepts reservations and credit cards.

The menu, for better or for worse, is not undergoing drastic change. The main choice, for knowledgeable habitués, is between choucroute (sauerkraut) and the daily special (which is often *bœuf mode*—stewed beef and vegetables). Americans still like to order the sausage in mustard sauce with potato salad—Hemingway's favorite.

- With whom: a recognized—and recognizable—celebrity.

- Where: 151, boulevard Saint-Germain, 6th. Tel.: 45.48.53.91. Opposite *Les Deux Magots.* Try to get the good banquette, and flatly refuse to go upstairs.

- When: every day until 12:45 a.m. Livelier at night.

- Recommended: the choucroute, *bœuf mode.*

- Welcome: more "democratic" than before; still excellent service.

- Dress: don't go for the shock effect: it's who you are that counts.

- Bottom Line: to see and be seen.

- Cost: 150 F.
- **Emergency alternative:** *Le Muniche*, 27, rue de Buci, 6th. Tel.: 46.33.62.09. Open every day until 2 a.m., but a lower status rating.

# Le Louis XIV

## Midnight

Porte Saint-Denis
Rococo

Le Louis XIV brings to mind the Madwoman of Chaillot rather than the court of the Sun King. The swirls of art nouveau woodwork, the tulip lamps, the fancy sconces, the funny upholstered garden furniture—it all looks like a set for the Giraudoux play.

Wealthy merchants from the garment district, visitors from the provinces, and hungry old bachelors drop in after theater. Before your eyes, an imperturbable cook skewers and grills pigeons, ducklings, and small chickens, but the restaurant is just as famous for its seafood.

The ravenous go for the big dish of fried sole, the platter of fresh pasta with seafood, and the profiteroles with pure chocolate; the more moderate opt for a delicate fish pâté with saffron, a grilled turbot, and poached pears with sorbet.

- **With whom:** small-town folks.
- **Where:** 8, boulevard Saint-Denis, 10th. Tel.: 42.08.56.56. At the corner of boulevard Sébastopol and boulevard Saint-Denis, between the two triumphal arches.
- **When:** from 12:30 to 2:30 p.m. and 8 p.m. to 1 a.m.; closed Monday and Tuesday.
- **Recommended:** friture (fried strips of sole), saffron mousse or fish soup, roast duckling, fresh pasta with seafood, profiteroles with chocolate, poached pears; Chiroubles.
- **Welcome:** well trained.
- **Dress:** bourgeois.
- **Bottom line:** a traditional after-theater supper.
- **Cost:** 200 F.
- **Emergency alternative:** *Julien* (p. 178).

# Le Petit Prince  ♥

## Midnight

Le Petit Prince—like the Little Prince of the St-Exupéry story—is finally happy. He's surrounded by friends who have come to pay a casual visit—easy-going couples of all ages and all manner of dress.

He shows them his collection of posters from the *Orient Express* and battered old spice boxes. In his disconcerting way, he has thought nothing of putting a bust of Louis XVI at the top of a staircase, which looks as strange and surrealistic as Salvador Dali's limp watches in the desert. And being a gentle person, he has gathered around him flowers, soft fabrics, and candlelight.

In this attractive interior, he'll suggest that you order an Indian curry or the After-Eight dessert. Dreamy. And even his down-to-earth prices seem unreal.

- **With whom:** a casual companion.
- **Where:** 12, rue Lanneau, 5th. Tel.: 43.54.77.26. Between rue des Écoles and the Panthéon, opposite the Coupe-Chou.
- **When:** every day from 8 p.m. to 12:30 a.m.
- **Recommended:** salad with lardons (diced bacon), curry or steak, After-Eight or deep-dish apple pie; Gamay.
- **Welcome:** delightful and efficient.
- **Dress:** elegant and discreet.
- **Bottom line:** for a quiet tête-à-tête.
- **Cost:** 120 F.
- **Emergency alternative:** *Le Berthoud* (p. 131) for dinner, *Dodin Bouffant* (p. 137) for a late supper.

# Le Sept

## Midnight

Rejuvenated, Le Sept has burst back in all its glory.
Black glass, mirrored pillars, and striated mirrors dance
with reflections, splintering images a thousand ways, as
in a Hitchcock movie.

This mainly gay group of night-owls lives in its own
little world, with past and present idols. One of them is
called, mysteriously, "the baron"—a haughty and solitary character to whom waiters, stars, and ordinary
customers come to pay their respects.

They chatter away in four or five different languages,
nibble the sophisticated dishes of a very "nouvelle"
chef, and make brief visits to the bar or to the pocket-
size club downstairs.

- **With whom:** a well-known dress designer or a
  lesser-known marquis.
- **Where:** 7, rue Sainte-Anne, 1st. Tel.: 42.96.25.82.
  At the end of avenue de l'Opéra.
- **When:** from 9 p.m. to 1 a.m.; closed Monday and
  Tuesday. Many evenings, there's a special "theme."
- **Recommended:** chopped avocado with Parma ham,
  papillote of salmon, fruit gratin.
- **Not recommended:** lemon mousse with kiwi sauce
  —too acidic.
- **Welcome:** pretty and perfumed.
- **Dress:** something silky.
- **Bottom line:** a dash of night madness.
- **Cost:** 200 F. for the fixed menu of the week.
- **Emergency alternative:** *Le Piano-Club*, just opposite
  (p. 225).

# Brasseries Forever

They seem perfect for a late supper: a few oysters, a choucroute, quick (if somewhat careless) service, a rather short wait for a table, and convenient locations all over Paris, near every theater, so it's easy to drop in after a show.

*Le Balzar:* 49, rue des Écoles, 5th. Tel.: 43.54.13.67. Right near boulevard Saint-Michel. Open until 1 a.m.; closed Tuesday. For a literary ambience after a movie. Calves' liver, tarte Tatin; house bordeaux: 150 F.

*Flo:* 7, cour des Petites-Écuries, 10th. Tel.: 47.70.13.59. Off faubourg Saint-Denis. Every day to 1:30 a.m. The warmest of all the brasseries in the Bucher chain. Come with your family. Alsatian foie gras or oysters, choucroute, sorbet; Riesling: 200 F.

*Julien:* 16, faubourg Saint-Denis, 10th. Tel.: 47.70.12.06. Near Porte Saint-Denis. Every day to 1:30 a.m. The favorite brasserie of tourists and trendy young men in convertibles. Foie gras, chateaubriand with béarnaise sauce, chocolate charlotte; Chaberlay: 180 F.

*La Lorraine:* 2, place des Ternes, 8th. Tel.: 42.27.80.04. Every day to 2 a.m. A showcase for the neighborhood bourgeoisie. Very convenient, after attending a concert at the Salle Pleyel. Pathetically slow service. Seafood, herring, choucroute, profiteroles: 200 F.

*Le Vaudeville:* 29, rue Vivienne, 2nd. Tel.: 42.33.39.31. Opposite the Bourse (the Stock Market). Every day to 2 a.m. Not far from the Comédie Française and the Opéra Comique. Mussels, sole, cassoulet, tartes: 200 F.

*Wepler:* 14, place Clichy, 18th. Tel.: 45.22.53.24. Near many movie houses. Everyday to 1:30 a.m. Calm and provincial. Closed Monday in July and August. Seafood platter, tartare, coffee parfait: 200 F.

# *Anagura*

## *Midnight*

There's a television set in a stuccoed cellar. All around, well-dressed Japanese businessmen are sitting quietly on a circle of banquettes. The sound has been turned off, but the video clip is subtitled, and one of the men, holding a microphone, is singing the words. The microphone is passed around, and soon it's your turn.

What do you want to sing? "Autumn Leaves"? "Love Me Tender"? Yes, they insist: you have to try.

Your first attempt will be pitiful. But everyone will applaud and pour you a shot of whisky, and little by little you'll get used to this game of "playback."

You're leaving already? Oh, no—sing it again, Sam.

- **With whom:** Someone with a good voice.
- **Where:** 13, rue Monsieur-le-Prince, 6th. Tel.: 43.29.99.14. At the end of the street, near the École de Médecine garage.
- **When:** 364 days a year, except for New Year's Day; from 7 p.m. to 2 a.m.—better after 11 p.m.
- **Recommended:** whisky (drinking sake makes you look like a tourist) and a plate of fruit.
- **Welcome:** surprised to see you there, but friendly very fast.
- **Dress:** high-stress executive.
- **Bottom line:** total immersion.
- **Cost:** 80 F.
- **Emergency alternative:** the Japanese bars on p. 197.

# L'Aviatic

## Midnight

First the Astaire (see below), now the Aviatic. A formula seems to be taking hold and fast becoming a real trend: corrugated sheet iron, aluminum pipes, and metallic lamps for a contemporary look; video clips as a background; a bar to liven things up; and the statue of a robot as an exclamation point.

People come here for brunch or to hang around at the end of the evening; it's a vague and casual kind of place well suited to vague and casual appointments.

Intellectual but easy-going, seemingly improvised but actually very carefully orchestrated, suddenly fashionable but sure to last, l'Aviatic has captivated me. I'm waiting for imitations to crop up.

- o **With whom:** a fashion designer.
- o **Where:** 23, rue Sainte-Croix-de-la-Bretonnerie, 4th. Tel.: 42.78.26.20. Closer to rue des Archives than rue Vieille-du-Temple.
- o **When:** every day from 10 a.m. to 2 a.m.
- o **Recommended:** the high-vitamin cocktail made with fresh fruit juice, "supersonic" ice cream, or mixed salad.
- o **Welcome:** seemingly cool, but quite efficient.
- o **Dress:** you can try out your latest look.
- o **Bottom line:** for a snack between two parties.
- o **Cost:** 60 F., on the average.
- o **Emergency alternative:** *Astaire*, 147, rue Saint-Martin, 3rd. Tel.: 42.78.83.50. And the latest: *Café New-York*, 68, rue Mouffetard, 5th. Tel.: 43.36.61.43.

# Le Bar Belge

## Midnight

The owner, a huge and magnificent woman with a crowning glory of a chignon, overpowers her little moustached boyfriend, who tries vainly to get a word in edgewise.

At the counter, old alcoholics and young men aspiring to that state catch up on the day's news, the races (horse and bike) and the local gossip, while buying each other rounds of beer from "the flat country" (Belgium).

This bar definitely has class: the boyfriend's stained white uniform is trimmed with gold braid. A photo of Belgium's King Baudouin hangs between pictures of the Mannekin Pis and Eddy Merckx, the Belgian bicycle champion. Jacques Brel would have felt at home here.

- **With whom:** Belgian friends.
- **Where:** 75, avenue de Saint-Ouen, 17th. Tel.: 46.27.41.01. Starting from Clichy, bear right at La Fourche.
- **When:** every day except Monday, to 1 a.m.
- **Recommended:** La Carolus beer or one of the Leffe brews (all Belgian) with a plate of cold cuts.
- **Welcome:** gruff and sincere.
- **Dress:** jackets with threadbare elbows (from leaning on bars).
- **Bottom line:** the temple of beer.
- **Cost:** 32 F.
- **Emergency alternative:** *Musical Box* (p. 193).

# Café Costes

## Midnight

Until recently the Beaubourg area seemed to be running out of steam. Its restaurants, once considered "in," were getting old. Its video bars were no longer fun. And there were no cafés in the neighborhood.

The Café Costes, strategically situated in front of the Fountain of the Innocents, looks to be a harbinger of better times. Its staircase sweeps upward before dividing in two under a big clock, similar in style to the one featured in an old Harold Lloyd movie. Upstairs, on the mezzanine, you'll come across an esoteric message, like a scrambled password. What does it mean?

The customers must know—they seem to be from the same tribe. Men wearing tuxedos, hippies with braided hair, trendy fellows with slicked-down hair, and the latest punks all merge here for a total look that's black, hard, and polished. From their hi-tech chairs, in a sudden burst of inspiration, they order a beer or a club sandwich.

- **With whom:** someone in black.
- **Where:** 4–6, rue Berger, 1st. Tel.: 45.08.54.39. At place des Innocents, at the corner of rue Saint-Denis.
- **When:** every day from 8 a.m. to 2 a.m. And sometimes, there are fashion shows.
- **Recommended:** club sandwich, soda, or beer.
- **Welcome:** self-consciously chic.
- **Dress:** New Wave.
- **Bottom line:** to see Philippe Stark's ethereal décor, the customers, the washrooms.
- **Cost:** 30 F.
- **Emergency alternative:** *Le Père Tranquille* (which *Café Costes* preempted), 16, rue Pierre-Lescot, 1st. Tel.: 45.08.00.34.

# Le Café Pacifico

*Midnight*

Montparnasse
Californian

The West Coast is "in." Even staid old Montparnasse has fallen victim to California chic.

American journalists, artists in heat, grimy truck drivers, and derelict beauties of the night now abandon the Beaubourg area just long enough to have a drink at the Pacifico.

They don't much care about the food—thick enchiladas and other heavy fare served on wooden boards. Rather, they come for the crowd at the bar, the best Margaritas in Paris, and the hair-raising shots of mezcal.

Don't be shocked if one night, carried away by the fumes and the rock music, a waitress in skin-tight jeans asks you for a dance.

- **With whom:** a serious drinker.
- **Where:** 50, boulevard du Montparnasse, 15th. Tel.: 45.48.63.87. Between the Montparnasse Tower and Necker Hospital.
- **When:** every day from 11:30 a.m. to 2 a.m.; opening time on Monday, 7 p.m. Happy hour from 6:30 to 7:30 p.m. Tuesday to Saturday. Champagne brunch on Sunday until 4 p.m.
- **Recommended:** Margaritas, mezcal.
- **Not recommended:** the food, and the Mexican sangría which smells like vinegar.
- **Welcome:** as at a college reunion.
- **Dress:** with your Walkman.
- **Bottom line:** a campus bar.
- **Cost:** 30 F.
- **Emergency alternative:** *Le Rosebud* (p. 195).

# Le Casablanca ♥

## Midnight

Video bars are nonsense. The novelty has worn off: the clips run on endlessly and tiresomely, their decibels drowning out all conversation.

The video frenzy that overtook rue Quincampoix has subsided faster than hula hoops. Le Studio (see below), with its Pompeiian decadence, is boring. L'Hallcatraz is as sinister as its prison namesake. Only Le Casablanca manages to hold on to its customers.

For in fact the place is truly conducive to a midnight rendez-vous, featuring a blue cellar that looks like an underground film show, service with a smile, and best of all, reclining banquettes that let you snuggle together while everybody is watching the big screen.

- **With whom:** a shy companion.
- **Where:** 41, rue Quincampoix, 1st. Tel.: 48.87.76.87. Between Beaubourg and boulevard Sébastopol. Avoid the restaurant.
- **When:** every day from 9 p.m. to 2 a.m.
- **Recommended:** tequila, the Scorpion cocktail.
- **Not recommended:** the Casablanca cocktail.
- **Welcome:** flirtatious.
- **Dress:** to blend into the darkness.
- **Bottom line:** for the video clips and the deep armchairs.
- **Cost:** 60 F.
- **Emergency alternative:** *Le Studio* (p. 117).

# Le Caveau Montpensier

*Midnight*

Too many establishments have thought that to create a pub one had only to serve Guinness on draft at a carved wooden bar, install some leatherette banquettes, and hang up a few ships' lanterns.

That's just not enough. Neither the Winston-Churchill, nor the London Tavern, nor the Cockney Tavern, nor even the Bedford Arms is really British. They're missing the strictly masculine clientele—the spirit of camaraderie and the warm jostling around the bar as mugs are raised on high.

The good news is that such a pub exists in a sparsely furnished cellar, unmarked and far off the usual Parisian circuits. Bankers from London, Cockneys passing through, and American journalists crowd around this warm, friendly bar, talking loudly, clutching mugs of Smithwicks, or challenging each other to a game of darts.

If you speak English, you have a clear advantage here.

- **With whom:** a man's man.
- **Where:** 15, rue Montpensier, 1st. Tel.: 47.03.33.78. Along the Palais-Royal, on the theater side.
- **When:** to 1 a.m.
- **Recommended:** a Guinness or a Smithwicks.
- **Welcome:** fraternal.
- **Dress:** comfortable, in order to play darts.
- **Bottom line:** for the beer, of course.
- **Cost:** 25 F.
- **Emergency alternative:** The other Irish pub, *L'Escale*, 55, rue Montmartre, 2nd. Tel.: 42.33.91.33. Even livelier, to the point of being a mad scuffle. They say the Smithwicks is served here at the ideal temperature. It's worth looking in one evening when a soccer match is on.

# Le Concorde Lafayette ♥

*Midnight*

High up in this cocktail bar overlooking the traffic at Porte Maillot, you're practically rubbing noses with the Arc de Triomphe and sitting cheek-to-cheek with the Eiffel Tower.

The banquettes are set into alcoves facing the view — which allows you to ignore the pretentious but inefficient service, the flashy decoration, and the equally flashy clientele.

Lovers, with Paris at their feet, seem nearer to heaven. And the slight sense of vertigo will only give them an excuse to cling more closely.

- **With whom:** a young, not very sophisticated, lover.
- **Where:** 3, place du Général-Koenig, 17th. Tel.: 47.58.12.84. On the 33rd floor of the hotel above the Palais des Congrès.
- **When:** every day from 11 a.m. to 2 a.m.
- **Recommended:** two cocktails: Barbotage's special (sweet) and the Spencer (dry).
- **Welcome:** not quite up to snuff.
- **Dress:** internationally anonymous.
- **Bottom line:** to show off Paris and set the stage. . . .
- **Cost:** 52 F.
- **Emergency alternative:** the same hotel, on the ground floor.

# Chez Georges

*Midnight*

*Saint-Germain*
On the road

Tramps drop in here to buy a bottle of booze, Chilean refugees come here to talk revolution, and old night-owls hang around dusting off their memories.

Georges has been on rue des Canettes for over 30 years. His customers spill out onto the sidewalk, lolling on car hoods or dancing around a hurdy-gurdy before returning to the French, Romanian, and other ethnic tunes emanating from the old vaulted cellar.

The anarchistic free-for-all is only a façade. Georges evicts any rambunctious druggies and alcoholics, warmly welcomes his faithful following, and soothes the overworked waiters with a few well-chosen words. You can't go wrong making a date to meet an old friend here, or some fellow tourists.

- **With whom:** a boozer, a tourist, or some old pals.
- **Where:** 11, rue des Canettes, 6th. Tel.: 43.26.79.15. Between Saint-Sulpice and boulevard Saint-Germain.
- **When:** from 11 a.m. to 2 a.m.; closed Sunday and Monday.
- **Recommended** (relatively speaking): kir, draft beer, or ordinary red wine.
- **Welcome:** brusque, but basically nice.
- **Dress:** a tattered handknit sweater.
- **Bottom line:** for the friendliness at the bar.
- **Cost:** 9 F.
- **Emergency alternative:** *Le Birdland* (p. 224).

# Le Harry's Bar ♥

## Midnight

Is this place American, like its founder, or Scottish, like its current owner? Perhaps Harry's Bar is simply a symbol of Parisian life, for generations of drinkers, literary figures, and good conversationalists.

In the great tradition of Hemingway, and his lost and found-again generation, Americans in Paris adore this noisy bar, where they hold their own presidential poll every four years on Election Night and rally around their college pennants. The British also have their school emblems to gaze at, as they crowd around the bar for a good draft, just as they would in any hometown pub.

Harry's Bar isn't an easy, outgoing place. It takes some time before you're known well enough to get through the bottleneck at the door. Make friends with the waiters, all of whom have worked here for more than 15 years. You'll eventually discover that you can also come here with female companions, to the piano bar downstairs, and drink a Blue Lagoon together— Harry's special creation.

- o **With whom:** members of the International Bar Flies.
- o **Where:** 5, rue Daunou, 2nd. Tel.: 42.61.71.14. Between rue de la Paix and avenue de l'Opéra.
- o **When:** from 11 p.m. to 4 a.m.
- o **Recommended:** Blue Lagoon and Bloody Mary (Harry's creations), 15-year old J&B, or simply a draft beer.
- o **Welcome:** tough the first time, then more helpful.
- o **Dress:** a jacket or a heavy sweater.
- o **Bottom line:** at the bar with men, at the piano bar with a woman.
- o **Cost:** 50 F.

- **Emergency alternative:** the bar next door, *Le Sherwood*, if you can't get into Harry's: 3, rue Daunou, 2nd. Tel.: 42.61.70.94. It's possible to have a bite to eat even at 4 a.m.

# Bar de l'Hôtel–Le Belier ♥

## Midnight

*Saint-Germain*
Beauty and the Beast
♈ ♈ ♈

In the great narcissistic tradition of l'Hôtel (Jean Cocteau, Oscar Wilde, and others of their ilk have preened
in front of the mirrors), Guy-Louis Duboucheron
flaunts his vanity. His name is engraved on the plaques
that grace the façade and the hall, his signature is
embroidered on the bath towels sold in the cloakroom
and on the pale-blue jackets worn by the waiters, and his
dazzling portrait hangs imperially over the piano.

The whole scene is bizarre: a parrot in an immense
cage, a tree-trunk in the middle of the dining room, a
monumental staircase under a glass cupola, a downstairs lounge decorated like a harem, a metallic ram, an
indoor fountain, and, everywhere, masses of flowers.

The luridly colored house cocktails are too ostentatious to be tasty: the Blue Moon is nowhere as good as a
Blue Lagoon at Harry's Bar, the champagne cocktail is
tart, and the Week-End is utterly lost. The only thing
missing at this strange bar is a really good bartender.

- **With whom:** an aesthete.
- **Where:** 13, rue des Beaux-Arts, 6th. Tel.:
  43.25.27.22. Opposite the Beaux-Arts academy.
- **When:** every day from 7 p.m. to 2 a.m.
- **Recommended:** be careful—just order a kir.
- **Welcome:** insufficient.
- **Dress:** overdone.
- **Bottom line:** amaze someone who doesn't know the
  place.
- **Cost:** 80 F.
- **Emergency alternative:** *La Palette* (p. 104).

190   LATE BARS

# Le Martial

## Midnight

All alone, Le Martial has perked up Pigalle. Like an ocean liner, it has three bars on board—one in the engine room for secret conversations, poker, and chess; another on the bridge for serious discussions; and the third in the hold, for the show.

The program is always surprising, even to the staff. It might be jazz, Birmingham rock, or cabaret. And from time to time there's a refined but very risqué striptease.

Watch out—sometimes the large black leading lady decides to choose a victim from the audience. It's fun to watch everyone panic—the hippies, the punks, the fashion slaves—as they try to avoid the invitation, either by ducking out of sight or avoiding her gaze.

- **With whom:** someone punk.
- **Where:** 26, rue Fontaine, 9th. Tel.: 42.80.04.57. Right next to Pigalle. Go to the bar upstairs, or the one downstairs with the show—at the risk of getting stripped.
- **When:** every night from 10 p.m. to 6 a.m. An impromptu rock concert around 1 a.m.
- **Recommended:** a Marvin Gaye (a dry, spicy cocktail) or a minty Vil Coyote.
- **Welcome:** the waitresses are students—friendly but inefficient.
- **Dress:** something leather.
- **Bottom line:** the last stop before Le Bus (see below).
- **Cost:** 80 F.
- **Emergency alternative:** *Le Bus Palladium*, next door (p. 223).

# La Mousson

## Midnight

The man in the trenchcoat approaches, puffing on a Chesterfield. She, sitting with legs crossed in a rattan armchair, stares back at him. The fan is humming, the wood shutters are clattering. . . .

La Mousson could have been the locus for one of those thrillers set in the tropics, where one anticipates a dramatic seduction scene at the mahogany bar.

Any of the wanton young women here certainly could seduce Bogey, but the cosmopolitan crowd that gathers at this popular bar is much more sedate. They prefer to hold hands and sip a foamy piña colada or a fruity, creamy Golden Dream.

- **With whom:** friends from the East, or beyond.
- **Where:** 9, rue de la Bastille, 4th. Tel.: 42.71.85.20. Between the Bastille and rue des Tournelles, next to Bofinger.
- **When:** the bar is open from 7 p.m. to 1:30 a.m.
- **Recommended:** piña colada, Margarita, Golden Dream (chock-full of vitamins).
- **Welcome:** stylish.
- **Dress:** designer jeans.
- **Bottom line:** to meet your friends, before moving on.
- **Cost:** 30 F.
- **Emergency alternative:** *Bofinger* (p. 167).

# Musical Box

*Midnight*

Maybe this is Toulouse-Lautrec updated for the video age. There's the same creative fervor, but journalists from *Libération* and young designers have replaced the old artists from Montmartre.

A pioneer and a survivor of the video-bar craze, the Musical Box celebrates pop culture by hosting exhibitions of young painters, live broadcasts of Radio-Montmartre, and shows of so-called alternative fashion where the clothes are auctioned off.

The ridiculous is made sublime. Kitchen stools and cheap plastic chairs look as though they've come from a thrift shop. The juxtaposition of an American pin-up calendar and a pinball table, of a stuffed monkey and a Betty Boop doll, make the place look like a surrealistic bazaar. But the cocktails, at least, are serious, and you can order the Greenpeace or the Gainsbourg Lollipop with confidence.

- **With whom:** pals.
- **Where:** 3, rue Aristide-Bruant, 18th. Tel.: 42.64.35.00. At the corner of rue des Abbesses and rue Lepic.
- **When:** from 9 p.m. to 1 a.m.; closed Sunday.
- **Recommended:** the minty Greenpeace or the Gainsbourg Lollipop, made with pastis.
- **Welcome:** rigorously informal.
- **Dress:** flower child.
- **Bottom line:** for a cultural exchange, of sorts.
- **Cost:** 40 F. for a cocktail.
- **Emergency alternative:** *Le Martial* (p. 191).

# Bar du Plaza-Athénée

## *Midnight*

*Alma*
Déjà vu

What's missing in Paris is a lively hotel bar, like Trader Vic's at the Plaza in New York. Perhaps the closest thing is the bar at the "Plaza" in Paris; it's depressingly British, but a good place to have a last drink before seeing your client home.

True, this retreat lacks a certain patina, the bar is cut off from the main room, and the syrupy pianist is boring. But the cocktails are first class, especially the house cocktail, made with champagne and a dash of raspberry syrup, and the piña colada, which for once is really frothy.

Sometimes this respectable bar actually loosens up — for example, when a long-haired rock group comes in for a noisy round of drinks before retiring to their suite.

- **With whom:** a business acquaintance.
- **Where:** 25, avenue Montaigne, 8th. Tel.: 47.23.78.33. Turn right from the lobby and go downstairs.
- **When:** every day until 1 a.m.
- **Recommended:** the house cocktail (champagne with raspberry syrup), piña colada.
- **Welcome:** proper.
- **Dress:** tie not required, but advised.
- **Bottom line:** for the last drink after a business dinner.
- **Cost:** 60 F.
- **Emergency alternative:** the bar at the *Hôtel de Crillon* (p. 9). Along with the Ritz — which is much too depressing — the only other bar that's fit to go to. Their Crazy Horse cocktail is great, but it's a shame the bar isn't farther away from the bustle of the lobby.

# Le Rosebud

## Midnight

Like Citizen Kane, the residents of Montparnasse have a Rosebud buried among their souvenirs. It's a bar at the end of rue Delambre, which is always smoky, noisy, and packed.

The waiters haven't lost their touch, in spite of the new pack of customers. You'll no longer run into the artists of the Paris School, but rather, witless adolescents who gather at night to talk about women while sipping a gin and tonic or a beer.

Don't come here if it's a romantic date: your tête-à-tête is likely to be disturbed. But on the other hand, feel free to join in the conversations of your neighbors.

- **With whom:** an artist in search of himself.
- **Where:** 11 bis, rue Delambre, 14th. Tel.: 43.35.38.54. From the crossroads of Raspail-Montparnasse, take rue Delambre toward the Montparnasse Tower.
- **When:** from 7 p.m. to 2 a.m.
- **Recommended:** a Pick-me-up, a gin and tonic.
- **Welcome:** speedy, high-handed bartenders.
- **Dress:** a long muffler would be appropriate.
- **Bottom line:** memories, memories.
- **Cost:** 40 F.
- **Emergency alternative:** *Le Select*, 99, boulevard Montparnasse, 14th. Tel.: 42.22.65.27. Always lively at midnight, and even at coffee hour.

# Le Satay   ♥

*Saint-Julien-le-Pauvre*

## Midnight

Drifting

♟ ♟ ♟

To experience India on the Left Bank—a fantasy of many a Parisian intellectual—is fulfilled by Le Satay. It offers them a wonderful winter garden in an Oriental setting—the better to pretend they've attained Nirvana.

Sipping a cup of Rêve du Nuit tea, they are enveloped by the glow of soft candlelight and the light that filters through the palm trees; sinking into the plush cushions, they are rocked by the haunting Indian music. Nothing is out of tune: the rattan tables go with the straw-matted floor and the deep-brown lacquer walls and ceiling.

And Le Satay drifts timelessly like a barge on the Ganges, to the great delight of all lovers.

- **With whom:** a young starlet.
- **Where:** 10, rue Saint-Julien-le-Pauvre, 5th. Tel.: 43.54.31.33. Opposite the church of Saint-Julien-le-Pauvre, facing Notre-Dame.
- **When:** from 4 p.m. to 2 a.m.; closed Sunday. The winter garden, set off to the right of the entrance, is for seduction.
- **Recommended:** satay, curry, fruit cocktail, Berthillon ice cream, Rêve du Nuit tea.
- **Welcome:** smiling.
- **Dress:** Valentino.
- **Bottom line:** tender is the night.
- **Cost:** from 30 F. to 100 F., depending on what you order.
- **Emergency alternative:** *La Passion du Fruit*, 71, quai de la Tournelle, 5th. Tel.: 43.26.04.02. And other similar, artificial paradises along the *quai.*

# Making the Rounds of
# Japanese Bars
## *Midnight*

In the evening after work, it's nice to get high with a group of guys. In Paris, as in Tokyo, Japanese workaholics let it all hang out in their favorite bar, but they prefer to do it among themselves. Foreign intruders—the "Gaijins"—are barely tolerated, and so you'll have to be very discreet, or be accompanied by a Japanese guide.

*Le Louvois:* 1, rue de Lulli, 2nd. Tel.: 42.96.59.13. Until 2 a.m.; closed Sunday and holidays. Worth seeing if only for its inoffensive air: a peaceful bar in an unremarkable building, and whisky to drown your troubles.

*Le Miki:* 3, rue d' Artois, 8th. Tel.: 42.25.26.78. Until 2 a.m., except Saturday. Welcomes the crème de la crème of Japanese expatriates and serves the very best whiskies at prices that correspond. An extra attraction, certain evenings: mah-jong in an adjoining room.

*Kappa:* 6, rue des Ciseaux, 6th. Tel.: 43.26.33.31. Until 11 p.m., except Sunday. A microphone is passed around the cellar for anyone who wants to sing in "playback." Good-humored ambience, and the snacks are famous.

And if you're very lucky, maybe you'll be able to penetrate the inner sanctum of another bar which is not known for an open-door policy:

*Akiko:* 5, rue de l'École-Polytechnique, 5th. Tel.: 43.26.06.24. Until 2 a.m. To sing . . . this time without a video screen.

# Let's Face the Music and Dance

## *Midnight*

What's there to do in Paris if you're bored with the private clubs and depressed by the big nightclubs? If you reject both the blasé showiness of the former and the formalized silliness of the latter? If you're not interested in Princess Stephanie's love life nor the AC/DC passions of fashion designers? If you no longer know whether Castel is bearable on Saturday night or if Nouvelle Eve has reopened? If you no longer want to be sized up by insulting, omnipotent doormen?

And what for? All these clubs on the Parisian circuit, old and new, have one thing in common: their perennial customers are bored. Tired of dancing, they parade their unhappiness. They come merely to be seen, have a drink at the bar, and leave. Even flirting seems outmoded.

However, if you're bent on having fun, don't despair. Go off the beaten track, let yourself get carried away by Africans, West Indians, Latinos, even the Chinese. Or, quite simply, go back to the places your parents' generation loved.

# Le Balajo   ♥

## Midnight

This is the kind of dance hall you see in old French films—and where you can still go to dance the old-fashioned way.

It's the antithesis of chic, the flip-side of the city, in spite of its décor (an allusion to the film *Metropolis*) of misshapen skyscrapers and dramatic lighting.

The music hasn't been updated. After a waltz, a tango, a foxtrot, and some novelty number, everybody catches their breath and waits for the next selection—maybe a bunny-hop or a conga line.

As luck would have it, Le Balajo has been rediscovered by rockers and teeny-boppers, who invade the place on Monday and Thursday nights. But over the weekend, the outdated dance hall returns to normal, drawing all its old faithfuls.

- o **With whom:** grandma.
- o **Where:** 9, rue de Lappe, 11th. Tel.: 47.00.07.87. Impossible to miss it.
- o **When:** Friday and Saturday from 10 p.m. to 5 a.m. For the rock evenings, arrive at opening time.
- o **Recommended:** beer on tap.
- o **Welcome:** casual.
- o **Dress:** wide bow ties, long sequinned gowns.
- o **Bottom line:** Monday and Thursday, it's for rock; Friday and Saturday, it's the last of the dance halls.
- o **Cost:** 70 F.
- o **Emergency alternative:** *La Boule-Rouge*, across the street, on the weekend.

# *Le Caveau de la Huchette* ♥

## *Midnight*

*Saint-Michel*
Conservative

Le Balajo is back in fashion, so why not Le Caveau de la Huchette? Here's a comfortable place that's true to itself and to our memories, featuring good, honest jazz.

Don't be taken in by its medieval trappings: phoney axes, miniature stained-glass windows, false coats-of-arms, and other plaster casts. Just get up and dance.

You'll be rubbing elbows with young people from good families, who are forbidden by their parents to go to discothèques; tourists who are finally discovering the last typical Parisian nightspot; a few jazz fans; and some Casanovas who appreciate the long, slow foxtrots.

There's fun for all at Le Caveau de la Huchette.

- **With whom:** someone who's not French, who's very young, or who is very nostalgic.
- **Where:** 5, rue de la Huchette, 5th. Tel.: 43.26.65.05. At the corner of rue Saint-Jacques.
- **When:** from 9:30 p.m. to 2:30 a.m., until 4 a.m. on Saturday and holiday eves.
- **Recommended:** a beer, rather than punch.
- **Welcome:** pleasant, except on Saturday because of the mob.
- **Dress:** proper.
- **Bottom line:** for dancing to jazz, and foxtrots too, if that's your thing.
- **Cost:** 50 F. to enter, 20 F. per drink.
- **Emergency alternative:** *Le Satay* (p. 196).

# Chez Gégène

*Joinville-le-Pont*
A charming country tavern

Right out of a Jean Gabin film, this place gambols along the banks of the Marne River, between a bowling alley and a miniature golf course. The eternal Saturday-night lovers, the waiters sweating under their tight bow ties, the red-faced dishwasher in a T-shirt—they're straight out of central casting.

It's very festive. The women are all dressed up in hand-knitted shawls and family wedding gowns; mounds of mussels and fries are washed down with strong red wine (Saignée d'Automne); and when the accordion strikes up an old tune, everyone gets up to dance.

Even the prices are old-fashioned. Imagine a mint cooler for only 8.05 F. As the ad says, in rhyme: *Chez Gégène, on y vient, on y est bien, on y revient* ("Chez Gégène—you come, you like it, you come back").

- **With whom:** a lacemaker, as in the movie of the same name.

- **Where:** 162, quai de Polangis, 94340 Joinville-le-Pont. Tel.: 48.83.29.43. Take the Metz autoroute and exit at Joinville. After the bridge over the Marne, take the hairpin turn on the right and continue along the Seine (which is again on your right).

- **When:** from noon to 3 p.m. and 7 to 10 p.m. Dancing on Friday and Saturday until 2 a.m., on Sunday from 3 to 7 p.m.

- **Recommended:** mussels and fries, squab, peach Melba.

- **Welcome:** hectic, but they do their best.

- **Dress:** jacket and tie required.

- **Bottom line:** to be incognito.

- **Cost:** 50 F. for the fixed menu, less than 100 F. à la carte. Cover charge for dancing: 75 F. including a drink.

o **Emergency alternative:** the place next door, *Chez Rob*. (No tel.) The bowling alley and the miniature golf course are also open at night. It's practically Disneyland.

# Le New Morning ♥

## Midnight

Faubourg Saint-Denis
Jazz loft

Now the best jazz club in Paris, this loft in the garment district doesn't dictate how you should behave. You can stand at the bar, stroll around, watch the wildlife, and even talk.

Unexpectedly, you'll find a very hip audience. Depending on who's playing, you'll see mobs of Brazilians or West Indians, cool types, real jazz aficionados, and even nonchalant cowboys hidden under their ten-gallon hats.

This place is always lively and perplexing, going from jazz to freestyle, from freestyle to the Flying Lizards, with detours into salsa and fusion. If you're not sure what time you're going to turn up, plan to meet here: your friend will never reproach you for having to wait.

- o **With whom:** "jazzmaniacs."
- o **Where:** 7–9, rue des Petites-Écuries, 10th. Tel.: 45.23.51.41. At the corner of rue Saint-Denis.
- o **When:** in theory, every day except Sunday, from 9:30 p.m. Telephone to make sure there's going to be a show the night of your choice.
- o **Recommended:** tequila served as it should be, Heineken's.
- o **Welcome:** nonexistent.
- o **Dress:** jeans and leather.
- o **Bottom line:** for the start of a nighttime outing; to get in shape.
- o **Cost:** 80 F. to enter, 20 F. per drink.
- o **Emergency alternative:** *Flo* (p. 178).

# Le Tango ♥

## Midnight

The most bracing black nightclub in Paris has opened in a shady neighborhood near Arts et Métiers. Rastas, Afros, and young trendies crowd in here, no longer for the tango, but for the wild, hypnotizing salsas.

A dense and multicolored crowd perspires profusely under totally ineffective ventilators. The humid, suffocating, equatorial ambience is faithfully reproduced, to the point that you feel you have truly earned your punch break.

Lovers know the merits of Le Tango—its sensual rhythm, its compelling promiscuity, its safe anonymity, and its air of licentiousness—and they now prefer it to the tiresome nightclubs with soft couches and langorous foxtrots.

- **With whom:** someone nice, who's looking for a change.
- **Where:** 11, rue au Maire, 3rd. Tel.: 42.72.17.78. From the Métro station Arts et Métiers, at the beginning of rue Beaubourg, to the left.
- **When:** from 11 p.m. to 2 a.m. It's better to come early—the place winds down after 2 a.m.
- **Recommended:** the punch.
- **Welcome:** chilly.
- **Dress:** safari suit.
- **Bottom line:** unexpected seduction.
- **Cost:** 70 F. to 100 F., depending on the day and what you order.
- **Emergency alternative:** *Les Bains* (p. 222).

# Weddings and Banquets,
# Chinese Style

## Midnight

*Périphérie*
Pearl S. Buck

This evening, how about catching Julio Iglesias in Chinese, as interpreted by a Taiwanese star in a leopard jumpsuit, performing in a shopping center? This, while attending a Thai or Chinese wedding, and dancing a slow foxtrot between servings of wonton and Peking duck. Paris's Chinese cabarets, not yet discovered, are well worth visiting.

*Le Capitol:* Centre Commercial Pariferic, 6, rue des Cités, 93300 Aubervilliers. Tel.: 48.33.61.11. At Porte de la Villette, on the other side of the périphérique (the ring road). Every day from 7 p.m. to 2 a.m. The most fascinating one of them all, in a sleazy neighborhood, with marvelous singers and a family-style welcome: 200 F.

*Le Tikoc:* Centre Commercial Massena, avenue de Choisy, 13th. Tel.: 45.84.21.00. Every day from 8 p.m. to 2 a.m. Saturdays are reserved months in advance because of weddings. The biggest restaurant in Paris, with the biggest gastronomic selection. It's La Coupole of Chinatown: 250 F.

*Dai Dong Kahn:* the same shopping center as above, but entrance on place de la Vénétie. It's the up-and-coming cabaret. Go on Friday and Saturday when Le Tikoc is full. It has the ambience of a supermarket: 200 F.

*Le Mandarin du Forum:* Forum des Halles, Level 1, 1st. Tel.: 42.97.52.46. The reliability and prestige of the Mandarin chain of restaurants isn't enough to bring Les Halles back to life. The competition is fierce in the Asian community: 150 F.

And also, *Le Palais de l'Est* (p. 211).

# After Hours

*Late-late Restaurants*
*Late-late Bars*
*Last-stop Nightspots*

# Le Restaurant du Palace ♥

**2 a.m.**

Grands Boulevards
Crazy

Formerly called Le Privilège, this place still suffers from delusions of grandeur. Inspired perhaps by Pompeii, it drapes its columns in shrouds and costumes its waiters in voluminous ash-gray outfits. Blame Garouste, the fashionable French artist, for the décor.

It's a theatrical world. Carnival hats, masks, and stage sets from the Italian Commedia del'Arte simply underline the restaurant's raison d'être: to amuse.

And it succeeds pretty well, attracting hipsters and models, gays and straights, and serving them food which continues to improve—no mean feat at this hour of night.

- **With whom:** some hip types.
- **Where:** 1, Cité Bergère, 9th. Tel.: 45.23.44.62. The little street just behind Le Palace.
- **When:** every day from 9 p.m. to 3 a.m. Reservations recommended on Tuesday, when there's a stage show.
- **Recommended:** *rillettes* with two kinds of salmon or orange salad, blanquette of coquilles Saint-Jacques with champagne, bittersweet chocolate cake or nougat ice cream; red Champigny.
- **Not recommended:** mixed salad with spinach and *fourme d'Ambert* cheese, *aiguillette* (thin slivers) of duck with kiwis, charlotte of (canned!) pears.
- **Welcome:** effete.
- **Dress:** nightclub.
- **Bottom line:** for a theatrical supper, before going to dance at Le Palace.
- **Cost:** 130 F., including entry to Le Palace.
- **Emergency alternative:** the restaurant at *Les Bains* (p. 222), not as good and more crowded.

208  LATE-LATE RESTAURANTS

# La Cloche d'Or

**3 a.m.**

La Cloche d'Or has always been a late-night attraction on the fringes of Pigalle, but for some time now this inn has deliberately existed in a time warp.

The heavy medieval style of the fireplace, the exposed beams, and the old lanterns: shades of Jean Cocteau! Autographed photos of singer Gilbert Bécaud, boxer Marcel Cerdan, and cabaret star Mistinguett also call up another era. And the owner is a natural for a film role as a Corsican crook.

But it all hangs together somehow, and La Cloche d'Or continues to be a good place to meet after theater or after a party. Join the crowd at the bar for a drink, have a tartare in the dining room, or yet another tête-à-tête in a booth upstairs.

- **With whom:** seasoned night-owls.
- **Where:** 3, rue Mansart, 9th. Tel.: 48 74.48.88. At the corner of rue Fontaine.
- **When:** serves until 5 a.m.; closed Sunday evening.
- **Recommended:** tartare, sweetbreads.
- **Welcome:** rugged and friendly.
- **Dress:** anything goes—from jeans to tux.
- **Bottom line:** for after theater, or after anything.
- **Cost:** 200 F.
- **Emergency alternative:** *La Brasserie Pigalle*, place Pigalle; open all night.

# Le Malibu    ♥

*Les Halles*
Tower of Babel

Of all the restaurants in the neighborhood, this African place is the favorite of the Chinese. Is it because of the delicious braised chicken, or the karate black-belt waiter—or simply the family-style welcome?

Blacks and Asians, mixed couples, ex-colonialists, and international night birds blend here easily, forming a sort of nighttime community within the wood-paneled walls.

The owner never stops laughing, while a tireless minstrel, clad in a caftan, sings his old refrain: "ça va, ça va, ça va."

- o **With whom:** an exotic friend.
- o **Where:** 44, rue Tiquetonne, 2nd. Tel.: 42.36.62.70. Near rue Étienne-Marcel, over the nightclub.
- o **When:** from 9 p.m. to 5 a.m.
- o **Recommended:** stuffed crab (served in a scallop shell), braised chicken, or beef *maffé* (with peanut butter sauce), mango for dessert.
- o **Not recommended:** "foufou" gumbo, watery ice cream.
- o **Welcome:** nice and relaxed.
- o **Dress:** vacation clothes.
- o **Bottom line:** a thousand and one nights.
- o **Cost:** 120 F.
- o **Emergency alternative:** *Le Babylone Tropic*, 34, rue Ticquetonne, 2nd. Tel.: 42.33.48.35. So kitsch it's funny, so rasta it's almost chic, and so reasonable you won't care how the food tastes. Also, *La Savane*, 7, rue Marie-Stuart, 2nd. Tel.: 42.33.83.77. A pistachio-green décor; famous for its honey-like "panther milk."

# Le Palais de l'Est

## 3 a.m.

Don't be fooled by appearances. The empty restaurant slumbering above the deserted tracks of the Gare de l'Est is just a façade. Upstairs there's a sparkling ice palace, swarming with Chinese revelers and lit by bright red and violet spotlights.

Singers from Taiwan, Hong Kong, and other exotic places, dressed in leopard outfits or décolleté sequinned gowns, intone the popular melodies of their country.

Some of the couples dance. But most of the customers barely hear the music; they're busy celebrating a birthday or a Chinese wedding with plenty of toasts, flashbulbs, and speeches. You'll order your own banquet of Chinese, Thai, or Vietnamese dishes—at this ungodly hour when the trains aren't even running.

- **With whom:** a crowd.
- **Where:** 186, rue du Faubourg-Saint-Martin, 10th. Tel.: 42.41.09.99. Between the Gare de l'Est and Porte de la Chapelle, above the tracks. Brush past the maître d' and go upstairs.
- **When:** until 5 or 6 a.m., according to the day. Find out in advance.
- **Recommended** (more or less): the complete menus for four or eight people; citronella (lemon) chicken, stuffed mushrooms; or forget the food and just have a house cocktail.
- **Welcome:** rapid-fire service, but pleasant.
- **Dress:** anything from an evening gown to a leather jacket.
- **Bottom line:** a fascinating scene, and food around the clock.
- **Cost:** 160 F., or 100 F. for the group menus.
- **Emergency alternative:** the other Chinese cabarets and banquet halls, if they're still open; otherwise, *Le Malibu* (p. 210).

# Le Square

*3 a.m.*

Le Square has a split personality: early evening, upstairs, it's bright, wood-paneled, and filled with young, fresh-faced types; late night, downstairs, it's dark, lacquered, and frequented by French pop stars.

It could be a stage: the leopard-print décor is wild, and if there are no celebrities one night, the customers take over like a band of troupers while the waiters strike theatrical poses, à la David Bowie.

They'll adopt you almost immediately, and will serve you lovingly prepared and beautifully presented dishes: puff pastry with asparagus tips, kidneys with wild mushrooms, a two-chocolate mousse, or nougat ice cream.

- **With whom:** show-biz people, after the show.
- **Where:** 6, square de l'Opéra Louis-Jouvet, 9th. Tel.: 47.42.78.50. Rue Auber, at the dead-end street between the Edouard VII Theater and l'Athénée.
- **When:** until 3 a.m.
- **Recommended:** Bohemian artichoke, kidneys with wild mushrooms, nougat ice cream, "tulipe" with two-chocolate mousse.
- **Not recommended:** picatta of chicken, lotte with vinegar.
- **Welcome:** charming and sensual.
- **Dress:** with care.
- **Bottom line:** for a nighttime romp, for supper after the opera, for the terrace.
- **Cost:** 200 F.
- **Emergency alternative:** *Le Persil-Fleur*, 8, rue Boudreau, 9th. Tel.: 42.65.40.19. Fastidious, attentive, and eager to please. A calm place for after-theater. Until 11:30 p.m.; closed Saturday and Sunday.

# La Tour de Monthléry

**4 a.m.**

You can't dance another step; it's time for a bite to eat. You don't feel like onion soup, so how about an onglet (a small steak) with shallots?

La Tour de Monthléry pays no attention to traditional, early-morning clichés; it caters, rather, to the tastes of the neighborhood butchers.

At dawn, this old bar seems surrealistic—with its hams hanging from the ceiling and its red-and-white checkered napkins.

But you'll quickly get the hang of it, and along with the others, you'll devour wonderful dry sausage, brains, or venison stew.

- **With whom:** big eaters, even at 4 a.m.
- **Where:** 5, rue des Prouvaires, 1st. Tel.: 42.36.21.82. Between les Halles and rue Saint-Honoré.
- **When:** day and night, except Saturday and Sunday.
- **Recommended:** sausage, brains, onglet; Brouilly.
- **Not recommended:** the desserts.
- **Welcome:** in shirtsleeves.
- **Dress:** as a night reveller or a night worker.
- **Bottom line:** defy the night.
- **Cost:** 150 F.
- **Emergency alternative:** *La Poule au Pot*, 9, rue Vauvilliers, 1st. Tel.: 42.36.32.96. Also for big eaters.

# Le 20 aux Halles ♥

## 4 a.m.

For some people—performers, restaurant owners, and night-owls—life begins at 4 a.m. Le 20 is their first stop.

The tall, effete fellow with sequins on his cheeks sets the tone for this uninhibited place: you can bat your eyelashes and carry on like a queen, but you're also welcome if you're a straight couple who just want to top off a good evening.

You'll particularly like the huge bouquets of flowers and the professional attentiveness of the waiters who don't force anything on you; it's a festive yet tolerant ambience.

- **With whom:** anyone who likes staying out late.
- **Where:** 20, rue Saint-Denis, 1st. Tel.: 42.36.67.77. In the part of the street that's open to traffic, on the rue de Rivoli side.
- **When:** until dawn.
- **Recommended:** fresh pasta or seafood salad, filet with pink peppercorns, ice cream.
- **Not recommended:** salmon with chives.
- **Welcome:** delightful and very open.
- **Dress:** androgynous.
- **Bottom line:** for a gay old time.
- **Cost:** 150 F.
- **Emergency alternative:** *Le 21*, directly opposite. Also open late, but not as lively. The address, naturally, is 21, rue Saint-Denis, 1st. Tel.: 42.33.56.27. Serves until 1 a.m.

# Le Pied de Cochon

## 5 a.m.

Some traditions never die. They just get handed down from one generation to the next. Onion soup at Le Pied de Cochon is among them.

True, *les forts* (husky guys who lug the merchandise) are no longer in Les Halles; they've gone the way of Baltard's old market pavilions, razed years ago; and the dirtiness of the neighborhood has given way to garbage of another kind. True, too, that Le Pied de Cochon has become, during regular hours, nothing more than a tourist trap in a setting that has been dramatically "restored" and gentrified.

But everything wakes up at 5 a.m., when the sun rises on the dome of the Bourse du Commerce. A fraternal spirit unites the revellers and the drunks, who clink glasses, shout at the top of their lungs, and dip into their neighbors' plates under the knowing eye of the maître d', who's used to that sort of thing.

Brave souls will order the pied de cochon or the famous *andouillette* (a pungent-smelling tripe sausage); the chic crowd will order oysters; and of course the traditionalists will order the onion soup. Served in a huge bowl, covered with a thick crust, it must be eaten ritually, in stages: first the soup itself, which rises through the crust after you've pierced it carefully with your spoon; then the cheese; then the croutons; and finally the onions. And, then, the party can resume. . . .

- o **With whom:** an inveterate night person.
- o **Where:** 6, rue Coquilliere, 1st. Tel.: 42.36.11.75. Next to the Forum des Halles, and the Saint-Eustache church.
- o **When:** night and day, day after day.
- o **Recommended:** the onion soup, the oysters, or, for the daring, the *andouillette*.
- o **Welcome:** like an old bistro.
- o **Dress:** end-of-the-party.
- o **Bottom line:** Perpetuate a Paris tradition.

- **Cost:** 33 F. for the onion soup, 133 F. for the seafood platter.
- **Emergency alternative:** *Vattier*, next door at no. 14 (p. 217).

# Other Late-Night Restaurants

A *tête de veau* (head cheese) or a country-style choucroute can be delightful at 4 a.m. Here are some suggestions for late-night moveable feasts.

## Food "Factories"

*La Maison d'Alsace:* 39, avenue des Champs-Élysées, 8th. Tel.: 43.59.44.24. 120 F. Hasn't closed for a minute since its opening many years ago. A very central location if you're in the Champs-Élysées area. Don't expect too much from the food or the service.

*Le Grand Café Capucines:* 4, boulevard des Capucines, 2nd. Tel.: 47.42.75.77. Open all night. Seems very proud of its Belle-Époque décor, which is rather flashy. Could do better with its onion soup. Great seafood platter.

## Around Le Pied de Cochon

*Vattier:* 14, rue Coquillière, 1st. Tel.: 42.36.51.60. Open all night. 150 F. A lifeless bistro; watery onion soup. Caters to some oldtimers.

*L'Alsace aux Halles:* 16, rue Coquillière, 1st. Tel.: 42.36.74.24. Open all night. 160 F. Tourists adore it for its ethnic music and the big family-style portions.

Also *La Marmite aux Halles*, 54, rue Jean-Jacques-Rousseau, 1st, and *Le Commerce*, 12, rue Coquillière, 1st.

## Night Workers' Bistros

*Le Duc de Richelieu:* 110, rue de Richelieu, 2nd. Tel.: 42.96.38.38. Until 5 a.m.; closed Sunday. 120 F. Smells of cheap wine; a little deserted early in the morning, but taxi drivers like it.

*La Nouvelle Gare:* 49, boulevard Vincent-Auriol, 13th. Tel.: 45.84.74.29. Open from 4 p.m. to 2 a.m. 60

F. A low-key, cheap bistro that attracts workers and taxi drivers.

*L'Épicerie Landaise:* 10, rue Princesse, 6th. Tel.: 43.26.02.96. 170 F. Open until 2 a.m.; closed Sunday. The drinkers and dancers from Castel, worn out from excessive nighttime activity, pull themselves together here, with solid cooking from the southwest.

And other emergency alternatives already noted: *Le Bar des Bains, La Savane, Le 20 aux Halles,* and *La Poule au Pot.* Night people definitely have an appetite.

# L'Ascot

*Champs-Élysées*
British

For 40 years the Ascot's customers have not been disappointed. They still can count on the perfectionist bartender (an expert gin-fizz maker), the romantic pianist, and waiters worthy of any proper English club.

Yes, the Scottish fabric is wearing out, the hunting prints are a bit second-rate, the stained-glass Derby scene is rather heavy-handed, and the equestrian fresco looks like a bad parody of Degas or Toulouse-Lautrec.

But to the Ascot's credit, it has stayed true to such old-fashioned values as comfort and courtesy. Delightfully outdated, it's reassuring to those gentlemen who want to be seen with their clients near the piano—or want to hide away with a girlfriend in the discreet backroom.

- o **With whom:** executives (of any level).
- o **Where:** 66, rue Pierre-Charron, 8th. Tel.: 43.59.28.15. Off the Champs-Elysées.
- o **When:** from 6 p.m. to 4 a.m.; closed Sunday.
- o **Recommended:** the gin-fizz, the Planter's punch.
- o **Welcome:** dignified.
- o **Dress:** a tweed jacket.
- o **Bottom line:** a timeless old bar.
- o **Cost:** 60 F.
- o **Emergency alternative:** the brand-new *Washington Square*, 47, rue Washington, 6th. Tel.: 45.63.45.10. Open from 7 p.m. to 2 a.m., on Saturday to 10 p.m.; closed Sunday. Vaguely art deco. And of course, after it closes, the *Keur Samba* (p. 227).

# Caveau de la Bolée

## 3 a.m.

At the witching hour, when students return to the Latin Quarter, do what Oscar Wilde used to do: knock at the door of the Caveau de la Bolée, identify yourself, and cross into the shadowy recesses of this gambling den. Join the chess players in their tiny cell, decorated by sketches of jesters and horses.

The players compete for money or honor, anxiously or stoically, intensely or jokingly. They drink Côtes-du-Rhône, not the bowls of alcoholic cider from which the place derives its name.

Who pays any attention to the guitarist strumming away in the corner, the solitary drunk muttering harmless gibes, or the newcomer who is thrilled to find a warm place in the middle of the night?

- **With whom:** a Grand Master.
- **Where:** 25, rue de l'Hirondelle, 6th. Tel.: 43.54.62.20. Place Saint-Michel, under the portal, toward rue Git-le-Coeur.
- **When:** from 7 p.m. to 4 a.m.
- **Recommended:** you're better off with the Côtes-du-Rhône than the cider.
- **Not recommended:** the punch.
- **Welcome:** not effusive, but appealing.
- **Dress:** jeans.
- **Bottom line:** for chess freaks—and, recently, back-gammon players too.
- **Cost:** 40 F.
- **Emergency alternative:** *Le Birdland* (p. 224).

# Le Gibus

## 3 a.m.

Don't smirk. Le Gibus may strike you as shabby, but at least it's honest. The sound system seems poor, but the music is pure. And although this dean of European rock clubs holds on faithfully to its fallen rock stars, it also takes risks from time to time. The Police, the Pretenders, and the Stray Cats all got their start here.

Le Gibus is open to everybody. It's like a vast parking lot, where you can either mix with the music fans, sink into the Chesterfield sofas, play pinball, or just wander around and check out the toughs dressed like dockers and the latest rockers in cowboy boots.

- o **With whom:** the rock generation.
- o **Where:** 18, rue du Faubourg-du-Temple, 11th. Tel.: 47.00.78.88. Right after place de la République.
- o **When:** from 11 p.m. to 5 a.m.; closed Sunday and Monday.
- o **Recommended:** scotch, straight.
- o **Welcome:** courteous.
- o **Dress:** slumming.
- o **Bottom line:** back to your roots.
- o **Cost:** 70 F.
- o **Emergency alternative:** *Le Palace*, as usual (p. 226).

# Les Bains

Beaubourg
Decadent

This nightclub, below street level under the cobble-stones of Beaubourg, is probably the last of its kind in Paris. It's where avant-garde photographers hang out, where fashion designers flaunt their latest creations, and where Prince was once inspired to give a private performance for his buddies.

It's steamily decadent, this Beaubourgian bathhouse, with blasé customers floating around like characters in a Fellini film. The women are beautiful but indifferent, clearly not interested in making an impression on, anyone. The T-shirted waitresses don't even bother to take your order. And the disk jockeys, in their graffiti-covered cage, are as spaced-out as everyone else.

The music—funk, salsa, and rap—is far more condu-cive to dancing than to chatting. This is the place for body language, not sweet talk.

- **With whom:** a friend from the underground.
- **Where:** 7 rue du Bourg-l'Abbé, 3rd. Tel.: 48.87. 01.80. Boulevard Sébastopol, at the corner of rue Turbigo.
- **When:** from 11 p.m. to 5 a.m.
- **Recommended:** nothing in particular.
- **Welcome:** nonexistent.
- **Dress:** whatever best reflects your state of depres-sion.
- **Bottom line:** the perfect place to exhibit your *angst*.
- **Cost:** 100 F.
- **Emergency alternative:** *Le Tango* (p. 204).

# Le Bus Palladium ♥

Thank God it's Friday. It's like Homecoming Weekend here. The gym has been decorated for the occasion, with cushions thrown around the floor, and pinball machines dragged onto the stage.

Everybody joins in and dances, including the teacher's pets (dressed in suits) and their dates (wearing sweaters with nothing underneath). The jeans-and-leather-jacket crowd will take over later on.

Le Bus no longer worries about what's in style. Its success seems assured — customers keep coming back. The music is really good without being far-out, the dance floor isn't too crowded, the bar is a bar in every sense of the word, and the comfortable sofas allow you to get closer at the end of the evening.

- o **With whom:** a college sweetheart.
- o **Where:** 6, rue Fontaine, 9th. Tel.: 48.74.54.99. At the corner of rue Pigalle, rue Fontaine, and rue Notre-Dame-de-Lorette.
- o **When:** from midnight to 6 a.m.; closed Monday. Sunday and Tuesday are the best nights.
- o **Recommended:** a whole bottle of champagne, if you can spring for it.
- o **Welcome:** an unpredictable bouncer at the door.
- o **Dress:** as you wish, formal or informal.
- o **Bottom line:** a classic nightclub.
- o **Cost:** 100 F.; 1,100 F. for a bottle of champagne.
- o **Emergency alternative:** *Les Bains* (p. 222).

# Le Birdland ♥

## 4 a.m.

The clientele next door, at Castel, hasn't the faintest idea this place exists. Birdland's customers are self-effacing, its decor unobtrusive.

Here, in this anonymous space capsule for night travelers, an inscrutable Asian bartender prepares his cocktails without a word, takes an order for chili con carne, and picks out some Armstrong, Bechet, or Coltrane from among his hundreds of original recordings.

Your last drink will stretch on and on, and you'll drift slowly down the river to New Orleans on a raft of blues or spirituals.

- **With whom:** an old pal.
- **Where:** 20, rue Princesse, 6th. (No tel.) Opposite Castel, near rue Guizarde.
- **When:** from 10:30 p.m. until dawn.
- **Recommended:** the chili con carne, a Smithwicks.
- **Not recommended:** the piña colada.
- **Welcome:** low-key but busy.
- **Dress:** patched jeans.
- **Bottom line:** get something to nibble, hear some jazz, and talk.
- **Cost:** 30 F. for a beer.
- **Emergency alternative:** *Le Bedford Arms*, across the street at no. 17. Tel.: 46.33.43.54.

# Le Piano-Club  ♥

Opéra
Generous

Le Piano-Club could be the setting for an Italian comedy, given its broadly sketched characters.

The bartender, like Harlequin in black and gold, no longer has time to prepare his much-appreciated croques-monsieur, he no longer deigns to mix cocktails, and he only serves one brand of champagne: Roederer.

The hostess, a red-headed Russian clad in an evening gown, flits from table to table, a huge glass of champagne in her hand. A true prima donna, her portrait reigns from the wall, and her extravagant floral bouquets remind you that in the madness of the night, you don't count pennies.

The pianist on the platform resembles Alain Delon, and doesn't seem to like the fact that he's providing only background music: his jazz riffs are terrific, as are his postures during the breaks.

- **With whom:** nighttime pros.
- **Where:** 12, rue Sainte-Anne, 1st. Tel.: 42.96.28.84. At the lively end of rue Sainte-Anne, opposite Le Sept.
- **When:** from 11 p.m. until dawn; better if you go after 3 a.m.
- **Recommended:** a glass of Roederer, possibly a whisky.
- **Welcome:** sophisticated, à la Dorian Gray.
- **Dress:** tuxedo or leather jacket.
- **Bottom line:** for those who like the night.
- **Cost:** 60 F.
- **Emergency alternative:** *Harry's Bar* or its neighbor (p. 188).

# Le Palace ♥

## 4 a.m.

♈ ♈

Le Palace is humming again, but at what a price! Fabrice Emaer, the original director, is gone, and with him, the crazy Palace nights. Also gone are the wild fringe characters—punks, toughs, and other rebels without causes. Once again this former theater has become a nightclub for well-bred young people, who dare to wear earrings and tight leather outfits only at night.

The décor is in constant flux: in the recent past you might have seen the imitation Crown Jewels, an enormous Max Ernst sculpture, or a Breathalyzer (which kids would try out as a precaution, before driving home in papa's Renault).

At dawn, however, when the real night people arrive, there's a little more action. Friends meet here for a last drink and reminisce about the Palace parties of yesteryear.

- **With whom:** a pack of friends.
- **Where:** 8, rue du Faubourg Montmartre, 9th. Tel.: 42.46.10.87. It's easy—right off the "grands boulevards."
- **When:** from 11 a.m. until the last person goes home. More interesting the later you come.
- **Recommended:** nothing special.
- **Welcome:** so-so.
- **Dress:** these days, very classic.
- **Bottom line:** your last stop, to hear the top songs.
- **Cost:** 100 F.
- **Emergency alternative:** *Le Keur Samba* (p. 227).

# *Le Keur Samba*                    ♥

## 5 a.m.                    The last of the last

Y Y Y

The night is already over . . . your usual place has closed. Will you now have to wander through Paris with the streetsweepers and milkmen? No, because it's just the right time to go to Le Keur Samba, for your very last rendez-vous.

In spite of the name, don't expect to find Afros and North African immigrants here. There are plenty of blacks, but they're African diplomats in tuxedos and evening gowns, millionaires from the Middle East who flaunt their Rolls-Royces at the entrance, and nightowls winding up their evening, slightly high or completely zonked out.

So what if the décor is flashy, with metallic palm trees and artificial flowers. Just give in to the rhythm of Afro-disco; when the work day begins, Le Keur will still be going strong—and so will you.

- **With whom:** a beauty of the night.
- **Where:** 79, rue de la Boétie, 8th. Tel.: 43.59.03.10. At the end of rue d'Artois, near Saint-Philippe-du-Roule.
- **When:** from midnight to dawn, and sometimes beyond that.
- **Recommended:** champagne, of course.
- **Welcome:** brusque.
- **Dress:** wearing a tie will help you get in.
- **Bottom line:** end of the line.
- **Cost:** 120 F., at least.
- **Emergency alternative:** for the first croissants of the morning, try *Le Champagne* at Porte d'Orléans, 14th, or *Le Café des Sports* at Porte de Saint-Cloud, 16th; but remember the hour and don't count on a very warm welcome.

# Salsa and Samba Until Dawn

*La Chapelle des Lombards:* 19, rue de Lappe, 2nd. Tel: 43.57.24.24. Actually, this place is a former prison, not a chapel, and the street name is Lappe, not Lombards. But it's the high temple of salsa, where the African and Antilles community of Paris come to dance, accompanied by the best bands from Spanish Harlem or the Caribbean islands. Don't plan to sit down. Entrance fee 60 F. Tuesday, Wednesday and Thursday, 75 F. Friday and Saturday. Closed Sunday and Monday. Drinks from 35 to 50 F. ♙♙

*L'Escale:* 15, rue Monsieur-le-Prince. 6th. Tel.: 43.54.63.47. One of the last cellars in the Latin Quarter —vaulted, minuscule, and suffocating—where night-owls dance sweaty sambas. Upstairs, Latinos calmly sip their Machu-Pichu cocktail to the strains of a harp and an Andean flute. Figure 60 F. ♙♙

*Chez Félix:* 23, rue Mouffetard, 5th. Tel.: 47.07.68.78. Go during the week, when it's not too crowded, to listen to Latin American bands. Stake out some room on the dance floor to do a tango or samba, or just sit together in a quiet nook in this maze of a cellar. But don't go during the weekend, when there's a sleazy crowd. Figure 60 F. Closed Sunday and Monday. ♙

*Phil One:* Parvis de la Défense. Tel.: 47.76.44.26. After wandering through the deserted, ominous-looking parking lots of La Défense (an area of high-rise office buildings west of Paris), you'll be happy to discover this loft, where you can listen to the best music from Africa, South America, and the Antilles. For 70 F., you'll forget you're in France. ♙♙

# Free - Style

# Cherchez la femme—the right place for the right woman

| MISSION OBJECTIVE | Identification (finding her) | New Horizons (something different) | Gazing into her eyes (reassuring her) | Other people (being seen) | Tête-à-tête (talking) |
|---|---|---|---|---|---|
| AN EXPENSIVE WOMAN | Brunch at the Hilton | Île de Kashmir | Robuchon | Lucas Carton | Le Jules Verne |
| AN INTELLECTUAL | Le Quatrième sans Ascenseur | Le Dogon | Au Rendez-Vous des Camionneurs | Lipp | Chez Marie |
| AN INGENUE | Tea at Cour de Rohan | Palais de l'Est | Le Gourmet des Ternes | La Coupole | Marshal's |
| A MARRIED WOMAN | Cocktails at the Raphaël | Le Baalbeck | Chez Guyvonne | Go to the next box | Les Fusains |
| A MODEL | Café Costes | Natacha | Olsson's | Le Potager des Halles | Cinnamon |

N.B.: If she's the love of your life, let passion be your guide—it's easier.

| MISSION<br><br>OBJEC-<br>TIVE | Hand in hand (touching) | The attack (urging) | "Let's stay friends" (leaving) | The ring (trapped) | The last straw (breaking up) |
|---|---|---|---|---|---|
| AN EXPEN-SIVE WOMAN | La Maison du Caviar | Le Grand Vefour | Chiberta | Taillevent | Mc-Donald's |
| AN INTEL-LECTUAL | Le Satay | Le Tango | La Coupole | Le Paprika | Chez Marius |
| AN INGE-NUE | La Truffière | Maxim's | Julien | Beau-villiers | A gay restaurant |
| A MAR-RIED WOMAN | Le Pavillon du Lac | Le Capitol | La Cafetière | In no event | l'Espace |
| A MODEL | L'Absinthe | A private club, then le Keur Samba | La Maison Blanche | Relais Plaza | Au Rendez-vous de la Marine |

# The Business World

| Stages | Objectives | Restaurants |
| --- | --- | --- |
| Making the first contact | Public relations | Le Divellec, Chez Guyvonne |
| Negotiating the deal | Space to work | Breakfast at the Plaza, lunch at Chiberta or at Restaurant de la Trémoille, or le Paris |
| Mounting tension | Showing your annoyance | La Lorraine, la Coupole at noon, a neighborhood bistro |
| The formalities | At last, it's serious | Taillevent, la Ferme Saint-Simon, la Maison de l'Amérique Latine |
| Signing the contract | Victory celebration | Lucas-Carton, le Bristol, le Pavillon de l'Élysée |
| Dinner with the spouses | Relaxation | Robuchon, la Maison Blanche, le Quai des Ormes |

If the deal falls through, better contact a head-hunter, and meet him at the Warwick, the Raphaël, or the Normandy.

# Visiting Paris with a Rich Uncle

## Panoramic Views

*Brunch* at the Hilton, *lunch* at Morot-Gaudry, *tea* at Flore-en-l'Île.
*Cocktails* at Jules Verne, *dinner* at Toit de Passy, a *nightcap* at Concorde Lafayette.

## Discovering Parisian High-Life

*Breakfast* at Deux Magots, the Crillon, or the Ritz.
*Lunch* at Taillevent, l'Espace, Bar des Théâtres, Récamier, Chez Edgard, or Pré Carré.
*Coffee* in the garden of the Musée Rodin.
*Tea* at Angelina.
*Cocktails* at Palette or Pont Royal.
*Dinner* at Robuchon, Maison Blanche, Chiberta, or Dodin Bouffant.
*Supper* at Lipp, Boeuf sur le Toit, Coupole, or Relais-Plaza.
*Nightcap* at Café Costes.

## In Search of Tradition

*Breakfast* At Cochon à l'Oreille.
*Lunch* at Petit Riche, L'Artois, Cinq Points Cardinaux, Jacques Melac, Reine Margot, Rendez-vous des Camionneurs, or any other casual place.
*Coffee* at Petit Fer à Cheval, Temps des Cerises, or Brocco.
*Tea-dancing* at Coupole.
*Cocktails* at Lloyds.
*Dinner* at Lous Landes, Gourmet des Ternes, Cochon d'Or, or Cagouille.
*Supper* at Louis XIV, Coupole, Cloche d'Or, Chez Jenny, or Flo.
*Dancing* at Balajo or Chez Gégène.
*Pre-dawn* at Pied de Cochon or Tour de Monthléry.

# Summer Outdoors:
# Terraces and Gardens

*Breakfast* at Deux Magots or Relais du Bois.

*Brunch* at Diable des Lombards, Mother Earth, Conway's, or especially l'Espace.

*Business lunch* at Récamier, Crillon, Morot-Gaudry, Flora Danica, Jardins de l'Élysée, or Hôtel Lancaster.

*Lunch with friends* at l'Entracte, Petit Saint-Benoît, Maison Rose, Ma Bourgogne, Reine Margot, Chez André, or on the Buttes-Chaumont.

*Quick lunch* at l'Espace.

*Coffee* in the garden of the Musée Rodin or in the Luxembourg Garden.

*Tea* at the Ritz, Muscade, Jardin de Thé, Grande Cascade, or Auberge du Bonheur.

*Cocktails* at Ledoyen, Père Tranquille, Tribulum, or Select.

*Stylish dinner* at Potager des Halles or Petit-Poucet.

*Charming dinner* at Maison de l'Amérique Latine or Beauvilliers.

*Dinner with a difference* at Studio.

*Celebration* at Gourmet des Ternes, Auberge du Bonheur, les Fusains, Pavillon du Lac, or Plateau de Gravelle.

*Midnight* at Café Costes.

*Supper* at the Square or Pied de Cochon.

# Sunday in Town

*Concert* at the Théâtre du Rond-Point, *mass* at Saint-Gervais, a *morning jog* or *shopping* at the open-air market on rue de Buci.

*Brunch:* **elegant:** the Royal-Monceau (including a swim), the Hilton, or any top hotel (for a traditional breakfast). **American-style:** Diable des Lombards, Mother Earth, Conway's. **High-brow:** Ébouillanté, Quatrième sans Ascenseur. **Fashionable:** Magnetic Terrace, Café Pacifico, l'Espace, the jazz brunch at the Méridien.

*Afternoon outing:* the Bagatelle gardens, an exhibition at the Grand Palais, or an old movie at the Cinémathèque.

*Tea:* la Cour de Rohan, Fanny, Carette.

*Dinner with a difference:* Chicago Pizza Pie Factory, Chinatown Olympiades, Studio, Dogon, Hawaï, Carr's, Sapna, Chez Gégène.

*Charming dinner:* Paprika, Maison du Caviar, or la Truffière.

*Stylish dinner:* Olsson's, Petit Poucet, Potager des Halles, Pupillin, Dave, Marshal's.

*Midnight:* any hotel bar, as well as Anagura, Martial, Café Costes, la Mousson, Dragon Élysées, Farafina.

*Late supper:* any of the brasseries, or the Relais Plaza.

*Special occasion:* any hotel restaurant, le Jules Verne, or la Cloche d'Or.

*Dancing:* le Bus Palladium, les Bains, le Capitol, Tikoc, and other Chinese banquet halls.

# Celebrations

*A birthday:* Chez Guyvonne, Palais de l'Est, or Morot-Gaudry.
*A wedding anniversary:* Robuchon, Lous Landes, Chiberta, or Au Quai des Ormes.
*Graduation:* Dodin Bouffant, Taillevent, or Récamier.
*Winning a sports event:* l'Artois or Petit Poucet.
*Winning an election:* Lipp, Récamier, or Coupole.

# Special Interests

## Intellectual

*Breakfast:* Deux Magots or Flore (for dissidents).
*Brunch:* Quatrième sans Ascenseur.
*Lunch:* Bar du Pont Royal (Gallimard), Balzar (Hachette), Temps Perdu (Le Seuil), Twickenham (Grasset), Chez Marie (Presses de la Cité and Laffont), Récamier (everybody), or Closerie des Lilas (oldtimers).
*Tea:* Fanny.
*Cocktails:* Pont Royal, Twickenham, or the Lenox bar.
*Supper:* Lipp or Balzar.

## High Fashion

*Breakfast:* Crillon or Plaza-Athénée.
*Lunch:* Relais-Plaza, Bar des Théâtres, or Blue Fox Bar. Designers go to Dave, Willi's, or Louis XIV.
*Tea:* Ladurée or Angelina.
*Dinner:* Beauvilliers, Olsson's, Natacha, or Cinnamon.
*Supper:* Coupole.
*Midnight:* Café Costes, Pacifico, or Mousson.
*Private parties:* Bains or Palace.

## Cinema

Sleep until noon, then *lunch* at: Pré Carré, Sormani, Extension 13, or Fouquet's.

*Dinner:* Potager des Halles, Pastel, Petit Poucet, or Da Graziano.

*Supper:* Square or Lipp.

While away the *night* at: Tour de Monthléry or 20 aux Halles. Wind it up at Keur Samba (with stars like Claude Brasseur).

## Television

Look for a producer at Bar des Théâtres.

Meet TV anchorpersons after the midday news at l'Espace, or at brunch at the Méridien.

Chat with folks from Canal Plus television at the Maison Blanche.

Have a drink at Sancerre, right near the Cognacq-Jay television studios.

Greet the network presidents at Pré Carré.

## Theater

Jean-Louis Barrault and his troupe at the Théâtre du Rond Point.

Actors and actresses from l'Équipe de l'Atelier at Kokolion.

Cast members from Théâtre Edouard VII and l'Athenée at Persil-Fleur or Square.

*Everybody* at the Cloche d'Or.

## Publishing

The top journalists go to Lipp, Chez Edgard, and Flora Danica.

Journalists from *Le Figaro* and *Le Nouvel Observateur* go to Louis XIV and Chez Georges.

Libération reporters go to Aux Négociants.

The *France-Soir* staff likes Chez Vong.

*Vogue* and *Vogue Hommes* people eat at Chez Marius.

*Le Monde* staffers go to Square or Grand Café Capucines.

Radio folks from station R.T.L. patronize Chez Edgard, while Europe 1 and R.M.C. have no special preferences.

# Customized Rendez-vous

## To Avoid Having to Make Conversation

*Breakfast:* Cochon à l'Oreille or Vaudeville.
*Lunch:* Cinq Points Cardinaux, Rubis, l'Entracte, Jacques Melac, l'Ecluse, or l'Espace.
*Cocktails:* l'Académie de Billard or Tribulum.
*Dinner:* Chicago Pizza Pie Factory, Studio, Café Max, Farafina, Baalbeck, Fortune des Mers, or Carr's.
*Supper:* Relais Plaza, La Coupole, Julien, or Chez Jenny.
*Drinks:* Café Pacifico, Caveau Montpensier, New Morning, Bar Belge, or Anagura.
*Late Night:* Palais de l'Est, Capitol, and other banquet halls.

## Where a Woman Alone Will Feel Comfortable

*Breakfast:* Crillon, Plaza-Athénée, Ritz, Flore en l'Île, or Relais du Bois.
*Lunch:* Cercle Rachmaninov, Rendez-vous des Camionneurs, Récamier, Bar des Théâtres, Blue Fox Bar, l'Entre Deux Verres, Rose-Thé, and the restaurants that draw a business crowd.
*Coffee:* Chez Basile, Verlet, or Musée Rodin.
*Tea:* Cour de Rohan, Fanny, Je Thé . . . me.
*Cocktails:* Forum, Pont Royal, or Ledoyen.
*Dinner:* Chinatown Olympiades, Dogon, or in the most quiet restaurants.

## When Your Friend Is Going to Be Late

**Panoramas and terraces:** See p. 96
**Lively places:**
*Breakfast:* Vaudeville or Deux Magots.
*Lunch:* Cinq Points Cardinaux, Rubis, Chez Edgard, Bar des Théâtres, or l'Espace.
*Tea:* Carette or Angelina.
*Cocktails:* Académie de Billard or Palette.
*Dinner:* Chicago Pizza Pie Factory, Olympiades, Studio, or Potager des Halles.
*Supper:* La Coupole, Boeuf sur le Toit, Julien, Lipp, or Flo.

*Drinks:* Café Pacifico, New Morning, or Bar Belge.
**Friendly welcome:** l'Entracte, Dave, Cagouille, l'Entre
  Deux Verres, Récamier, Lloyds, or Café Max.
**Reading your newspaper:**
*Breakfast:* Domaines, Flore en l'Île, Je Thé . . . me,
  Fanny Tea, Société Théosophique de France, Lloyds,
  or Blue Fox Bar.

## Discreet Rendez-vous

*Breakfast:* Cinq Points Cardinaux, Au Rendez-vous de la
  Marine, Extension 13, Restaurant de la Trémoille.
*Offbeat tea:* Je Thé . . . Me or Société Théosophique de
  France.
*Out-of-the-way bars:* Warwick, Normandy, Raphaël,
  Lenox, or Bar Belge.
*Dinners with a difference:* Haynes, Dogon, Olym-
  piades, Paprika, or Carr's.
*Supper:* le Kokolion.
*Dancing:* Capitol and other Chinese banquet halls, or le
  Gibus.

## Extravagant Rendez-vous

*Breakfast:* Crillon, Cochon à l'Oreille, or Relais du Bois.
*Lunch:* l'Espace, Rose des Sables, Cinq Points
  Cardinaux, Extension 13, Pré Carré.
*Coffee:* Temps des Cerises.
*Tea:* Société Théosophique de France.
*Dinner with a difference:* for charm, Maison de
  l'Amérique Latine or Maxim's: for sheer luxury,
  Beauvilliers or Robuchon.
*Midnight:* l'Hôtel (le Belier).
*Supper:* Boeuf sur le Toit.
*Late night:* Palais de l'Est and other Chinese cabarets,
  Piano-Club, or Caveau de la Bolée.

## Rendez-vous on a Budget

*Breakfast:* Cochon à l'Oreille or Vaudeville.
*Lunch:* Cinq Points Cardinaux, Rendez-vous de la Ma-
  rine, and other restaurants near the Arsenal,
  Trumilou, Cercle Rachmaninov, Rendez-vous des
  Camionneurs, Commerce aux Deux Marches, or
  Jacques Melac.
*Coffee:* Temps des Cerises.
*Cocktails:* Bar du Marais, Bar Belge, or Lloyds.
*Dinner:* Chicago Pizza Pie Factory or Farafina.

*Midnight:* Caveau Montpensier, Chez Georges, or Caveau de la Huchette.
*Supper:* Chez Jenny.
*Late night:* Caveau de la Bolée, Tour de Monthléry, Birdland, or Chez Gégène.

*Three stars for the price of one:* Enjoy these top restaurants at *lunchtime,* when there's a special low-price menu: Le Divellec, La Ferme Saint-Simon, Le Grand Vefour, Le Jules Verne, La Maison Blanche, Morot-Gaudry, La Tour d'Argent.

# Special Needs

# After the theater

| AREA | THEATER | BRASSERIE | INTIMATE | SHOW BIZ |
|---|---|---|---|---|
| CHAMPS-ÉLYSÉES | Chaillot, Renaud-Barrault, Théâtre des Champs-Élysées Pleyel, and Gaveau. | Le Boeuf sur le Toit | La Maison du Caviar I and II, or Les Innocents | Théâtre du Rond-Point, l'Espace, or Olsson's |
| OPÉRA | Opéra, Opéra Comique, Édouard VII, Daunou | Grand Café Capucine | Au Petit Riche | Le Square |
| PALAIS-ROYAL | Théâtre du Palais Royal, Comédie Française | Le Vaudeville | L'Entracte | Le Sept |
| CHÂTELET | Théâtre de la Ville, T.M.P. | Brasserie de l'Île | Le 20 aux Halles | La Tour de Monthléry |
| GRANDS BOULEVARDS | Théâtres de Boulevard | Julien | Louis XIV | Flo |
| MONTMARTRE | L'Atelier, and around Pigalle | Wepler | Le Pupillin | Le Kokolion |
| MONTPARNASSE | Theaters on rue de la Gaité | La Coupole | Natacha | Café Pacifico |
| SAINT-GERMAIN-ODÉON | Théâtre de l'Odéon, Alcazar | Lipp | Chez Marie | Dodin Bouffant |

# After a movie

| Neighborhood | After the early show | After the late show |
|---|---|---|
| Champs-Élysées | Fouquet's | Olsson's |
| Montparnasse | Le Select | La Coupole |
| Saint-Germain | La Cafetière | Lipp |
| Saint-Michel | Cour de Rohan | Le Balzar |
| Opéra | Pandora | Le Square |
| Clichy | L'Académie de Billard | Wepler |
| Cinémathèque | Carette | Bar des Théâtres |

# After a museum visit

*Louvre, Arts décoratifs:* Angelina, Le Meurice.
*Grand et Petit Palais:* Ledoyen, Ladurée.
*Beaubourg:* Le Jardin de Thé.
*Palais de Tokyo:* Carette.
*Centre Culturel du Marais:* Quatrième sans Ascenseur.

# While shopping

*On faubourg St.-Honore:* Ladurée.
*Au Printemps, Galeries Lafayette:* Croque la Lune.
*B.H.V., Samaritaine:* Fanny Tea.
*Arcades de Rivoli:* Le Meurice, Angelina.
*Around the Opéra:* Pandora.

# While antique-hunting

*Around the Louvre:* Rose Thé.
*Around rue du Cherche-Midi:* Le Recamier.

# While gallery hopping

*Left Bank:* La Palette.
*Avenue Matignon, faubourg Saint-Honoré:* Ladurée.
*Beaubourg:* le Jardin de Thé.

# List of Restaurants
# By Arrondissement

## 1st arrondissement

**9 a.m.:** Café Costes p. 14; Le Ritz p. 12; **Noon:** Au Rendez-vous des Camionneurs p. 38; Le Caveau du Palais p. 39; Conway's p. 22; Le Dauphin p. 40; Le Diable des Lombards p. 22; L'Entracte p. 30; La Gaudriole p. 30; Magnetic Terrace p. 21; Mother Earth p. 22; Le Rubis p. 40; **1 p.m.:** Le Grand Vefour p. 49; Le Potiron p. 74; Rose Thé p. 74; Willi's p. 75; **3 p.m.:** Muscade p. 96; Ritz p. 96; Verlet p. 84; **5 p.m.:** Angelina p. 95; Fanny Tea p. 90; Le Meurice p. 95; Toraya p. 94; W. H. Smith & Son p. 95; **7 p.m.:** Le Tribulum p. 105; **9 p.m.:** L'Absinthe p. 118; Les Boucholeurs p. 132; Carr's p. 111; **10 p.m.:** Chez Vong p. 159; Dave p. 151; Elmo Coppi p. 151; Le Potager des Halles p. 159; **Midnight:** Café Costes p. 182; Le Casablanca p. 184; Le Caveau Montpensier p. 185; Gourmard p. 166; Le Mandarin du Forum p. 205; Le Père Tranquille p. 182; Le Sept p. 177; **4 a.m.:** L'Alsace aux Halles p. 217; Le Commerce p. 217; La Marmite aux Halles p. 217; Le Piano-Club p. 225; La Poule au Pot p. 213; La Tour de Monthlèry p. 213; Le 20 aux Halles p. 214; Le 21 p. 214; Vattier p. 217; **5 a.m.:** Le Cochon à L'Oreille p. 4; Le Pied de Cochon p. 215;

## 2nd arrondissement

**8 a.m.:** Le Vaudeville p. 8; **Noon:** L'Entre Deux Verres p. 31; Pandora p. 21, 97; **1 p.m.:** Chez Georges p. 75; **9 p.m.:** Aasha p. 116; **Midnight:** L'Escale p. 185; Le Harry's Bar p. 188; Le Louvois p. 197; Le Sherwood p. 189; Le Vaudeville p. 178; **3 a.m.:** Le Babylone Tropic p. 210; Le Malibu p. 210; La Savane p. 210; **4 a.m.:** Le Duc de Richelieu p. 217; Le Grand Café Capucines p. 217;

## 3rd arrondissement

**3 p.m.:** Brocco p. 80; **10 p.m.:** Janou p. 152; Le Pastel p. 157; **Midnight:** Astaire p. 180; Jenny p. 171; Le Tango p. 204; **3 a.m.:** Les Bains p. 222;

## 4th arrondissement

**10 a.m.:** Le Flore en l'Île p. 13; **Noon:** Brasserie du Pont-Louis-Philippe p. 41; L'Ébouillanté p. 16; Le Quatrième sans Ascenseur p. 21; Le Trumilou p. 41; **3 p.m.:** Au Petit Fer à Cheval p. 82; Jardin de Thé p. 96; Le Temps des Cerises p. 83; **9 p.m.:** Au Quai des Ormes p. 144; Farafina p. 113; Le Studio p. 117; **10 p.m.:** Ma Bourgogne p. 152; Pacific Palisades p. 157; **Midnight:** L'Aviatic p. 180; Bofinger p. 167; La Brasserie de L'Île Saint-Louis p. 168; Café Costes p. 182; La Mousson p. 192; L'Orangerie p. 168; Le Pére Tranquille p. 182;

## 5th arrondissement

**9 a.m.:** Sweet et Faim p. 13; **1 p.m.:** La Tour d'Argent p. 49; **9 p.m.:** Le Berthoud p. 131; Bofinger p. 137; Dodin Bouffant p. 137; Le Paprika p. 115; La Truffiére p. 129; **Midnight:** Akiko p. 197; Le Balzar p. 178; Café New-York p. 180; Le Caveau de la Huchette p. 200; La Passion du Fruit p. 196; Le Petit Prince p. 176; Le Satay p. 196;

## 6th arrondissement

**8 a.m.:** Les Deux Magots p. 6; Le Flore p. 7; **11 a.m.:** Art et Buffet p. 21; **Noon:** Polidor p. 36; **1 p.m.:** Le Cherche-Midi p. 59; Chez Guy p. 20; La Marlotte p. 66; Le Paris p. 53; **3 p.m.:** Café de la Mairie p. 79; **5 p.m.:** La Cour de Rohan p. 89; **7 p.m.:** La Palette p. 104; Le Twickenham p. 100; **9 p.m.:** Le Bougnat p. 120; La Cafetière p. 133; Chez Marie p. 126; Le Temps Perdu p. 133; **10 p.m.:** Cinnamon p. 149; Petit Saint-Benoît p. 149; **Midnight:** Anagura p. 179; Bar de l'Hôtel-le Belier p. 190; Chez Georges p. 187; Kappa p. 197; Lipp p. 173; Le Muniche p. 174; **3 a.m.:** Caveau de la Bolée p. 220; Washington Square p. 219; **4 a.m.:** Le Bedford Arms p. 224; Le Birdland p. 224; L'Épicerie Landaise p. 218;

## 7th arrondissement

**Noon:** La Reine Margot p. 37; Le Sancerre p. 37; **1 p.m.:** Chez Françoise p. 65; Chez Marius p. 65; Le Divellec p. 45; La Ferme Saint-Simon p. 44; Les Glénan p. 65; Le Récamier p. 58; **3 p.m.:** La Buvette du Musée Rodin p. 81; Chez Basile p. 78; Christian Constant p. 79; Pradier p. 81; **5 p.m.:** Le Petit Boule p. 92; Société Théosophique de France p. 92; **7 p.m.:** Bar du Pont Royal p. 100; **9 p.m.:** Le Jules Verne p. 122; Maison de l'Amerique Latine p. 124; L'Oeillade p. 124; **10 p.m.:** L'Auberge Bressane p. 148; Café Max p. 148;

## 8th arrondissement

**8 a.m.:** Les Domaines p. 14; **8:30 a.m.:** Ladurée p. 97; **9 a.m.:** Le Bristol p. 9; Le George-V p. 10; Hôtel de Crillon p. 9; Le Plaza Athénée p. 10; **11:30 a.m.:** Croque la Lune p. 97; **Noon:** L'Artois p. 24; Chez Germain p. 25; L'Espace p. 21; Royal-Monceau p. 18; **1 p.m.:** Au Mandarin p. 69; Le Bar des Théâtres p. 67; Le Blue Fox Bar p. 68; Le Bristol p. 43; La Cascade Chinoise p. 69; Chez André p. 46; Chez Edgard p. 46; Chez Pepita p. 67; Dragons-Élysée p. 69, L'Écluse p. 70; L'Espace p. 73; Extension 13 p. 48; Fauchon (cafeteria) p. 68; Flora Danica p. 61; Hôtel Lancaster p. 64; Laurent p. 54; Lucas-Carton p. 50; Marius et Jeannette p. 51; Le Pavillon de l'Élysée p. 54; Le Relais Plaza p. 60; Restaurant de la Trémoille p. 64; La Rose des Sables p. 61; Taillevent p. 63; Théâtre du Rond-Point p. 71, 73; **7 p.m.:** Le Forum p. 101; Fouquet's p. 102; Ledoyen p. 102; Le Lloyds p. 103; **9 p.m.:** Chiberta p. 136; The Chicago Pizza Pie Factory p. 108; City Rock Café p. 108; Le Gourmet des Ternes p. 139; Les Innocents p. 130; La Maison du Caviar p. 125; Maxim's p. 127; Safari Club p. 125; **10 p.m.:** La Fermette Marbeuf p. 156; Marshal's p. 153; Olsson's p. 155; **Midnight:** Bar du Plaza-Athenée p. 194; Le Boeuf sur le Toit p. 166; La Lorraine p. 178; Le Miki p. 197; **3 a.m.:** L'Ascot p. 219; **4 a.m.:** La Maison d'Alsace p. 217; **5 a.m.:** Le Keur Samba p. 227;

## 9th arrondissement

**8 a.m.:** Café de la Pain p. 8; Le Grand Hôtel p. 12; **1 p.m.:** Au Petit Riche p. 55; Le Saintongeais p. 55; **7 p.m.:** Academie de Billard de Clichy-Montmartre p. 98; Cockney Tavern p. 99; **9 p.m.:** Anarkali p. 114; Haynes p. 114; **10 p.m.:** Le Pupillin p. 160; **Midnight:** Le Martial p. 191; **2 a.m.:** Le Restaurant du Palace p. 208; **3 a.m.:** Le Bus Palladium p. 223; La Cloche d'Or p. 209; Le Persil-Fleur p. 212; Le Square p. 212; **4 a.m.:** Le Palace p. 226;

## 10th arrondissement

**7 a.m.:** Le Terminus Nord p. 5; **9 a.m.:** Le Grand Hôtel p. 12; **1 p.m.:** Le Symbole p. 62; **9 p.m.:** Le Baalbeck p. 110; Le Dogon p. 112; **Midnight:** Flo p. 178; Chez

Julien p. 178; Le Louis XIV p. 175; Le New Morning p. 203; **3 a.m.:** Le Palais de l'Est p. 211;

## 11th and 12th arrondissements

**Noon:** À Sousceyrac p. 32; Chez Paul p. 35; Les Cinq Points Cardinaux p. 28; Jacques Melac p. 32; Restaurant Antoine p. 36; **Midnight:** Le Balajo p. 199; La Boule-Rouge p. 199; **3 a.m.:** Le Gibus p. 221; **9 p.m.:** Le Petit Chartier p. 113; Restaurant du Plateau de Gravelle p. 145; Sapna p. 116;

## 13th, 14th, and 15th arrondissements

**8 a.m.:** Le Dôme p. 14; **9 a.m.:** Les Jardins de la Paresse p. 22; **11 a.m.:** Hilton p. 15; **11:30 a.m.:** Macadam p. 20; **1 p.m.:** La Gauloise p. 65; Morot-Gaudry p. 52; **5 p.m.:** Thé Dansant at La Coupole p. 93; Je Thé . . . me p. 91; **8 p.m.:** Chinatown Olympiades p. 109; Hawaî p. 109; **9 p.m.:** Bermuda Onion p. 146; La Closerie des Lilas p. 126; La Cogouille p. 134; Le Duc p. 142; La Fortune des Mers p. 135; Lous Landes p. 142; La Maison Blanche p. 143; **10 p.m.:** Le Commerce p. 162; Natacha p. 154; Le Volant p. 162; **Midnight:** Le Café Pacifico p. 183; La Coupole p. 170; Dai Dong Kahn p. 205; Le Dôme p. 170; Le Rosebud p. 195; Le Select p. 195; Le Tikoc p. 205; **4 a.m.:** Le Champagne p. 227; La Nouvelle Gare p. 217;

## 16th arrondissement

**9 a.m.:** Le Pub Winston Churchill p. 11; La Résidence du Bois p. 11; **Noon:** Cercle Musicale Rachmaninov p. 27; Thé Cool p. 21, 97; **4 p.m.:** L'Auberge du Bonheur p. 96; La Grande Cascade p. 96; **5 p.m.:** Carette p. 88; Coquelin Ainé p. 88; L'Étoile p. 93; Le Chalet des Îles p. 145; **9 p.m.:** Café Mexico p. 146; Île de Kashmir p. 121; Le Relais du Bois p. 145; Robuchon p. 141; Le Shogun p. 121; Le Toit de Passy p. 123; Le Totem p. 145; **10 p.m.:** Le Restaurant des Chauffeurs p. 161; Le XVI p. 161; **4 a.m.:** Le Cafe des Sports;

## 17th arrondissement

**9 a.m.:** Le Stubli p. 14; **Noon:** Méridien p. 17; **1 p.m.:** L'Entrécôte p. 72; Le Manoir de Paris p. 44; Le Petit Salé p. 72; Le Pré Carré p. 56; Sormani p. 56; **9 p.m.:** Apicus p. 143; Chez Guyvonne p. 140; Il était une oie dans le

Sud-Ouest p. 139; Petrus p. 140; Rech p. 139; **Midnight:** Le Bar Belge p. 181; Le Concorde Lafayette p. 186;

## 18th arrondissement

**7 a.m.:** Le Terrass Hôtel p. 14; **Noon:** Aux Négociants p. 26; Au Tournant de la Butte p. 34; Au Virage Lepic p. 34; La Maison Rose p. 34; **9 p.m.:** Beauvilliers p. 119; Le Clodenis p. 138; Fouta Toro p. 112; Les Fusains p. 138; **10 p.m.:** Da Graziano p. 150; **Midnight:** Le Kokolion p. 172; Musical Box p. 193; La Pomponnette p. 178; Wepler p. 178;

## 19th arrondissement

**Noon:** Au Bon Accueil de Seine-et-Marne p. 29; Au Rendez-vous de la Marine p. 29; Au Rendez-vous du Port p. 29; Pavillon du Lac p. 42; Les Salons Weber p. 42;

## Nearby suburbs:

**9 p.m.: Neuilly:** Café de la Jatte p. 146; **10 p.m.: Neuilly:** La Guinguette de Neuilly p. 158; Le Petit Poucet p. 158; Les Pieds dans l'Eau p. 158; **Janville-le-Pont:** Chez Gégène p. 201; Chez Rob p. 202; **Midnight: Aubervilliers:** Le Capitol p. 205.

# Index

## W